böhlau

Legal Area Studies

Edited by
Martin Löhnig

Volume 2

Martin Löhnig / Ivelina Masheva (eds.)

Commercial Law in Southeastern Europe

Legislation and Jurisdiction from Tanzimat Times until the Eve of the Great War

BÖHLAU VERLAG WIEN KÖLN

Bibliographic information published by the Deutsche Nationalbibliothek:
The Deutsche Nationalbibliothek lists this publication in the Deutsche Nationalbibliografie; detailed bibliographic data available online: https://dnb.de.

Cover image: *Le Petit Journal* on the Bosnian Crisis (1908): Bulgaria declares its independence and its prince Ferdinand is named Tsar, Austria-Hungary, in the person of Emperor Francis Joseph, annexes Bosnia and Herzegovina, while the Ottoman Sultan Abdul Hamid II looks on helplessly. Unknown artist.

Cover design: Michael Haderer, Vienna
Proofreading: Dominic Joseph Bielby, Regensburg
Typesetting: le-tex publishing services, Leipzig

Printed and bound: Hubert & Co. BuchPartner, Göttingen
Printed in the EU

Vandenhoeck & Ruprecht Verlage | www.vandenhoeck-ruprecht-verlage.com
ISBN 978-3-205-21291-1

Contents

Abbreviations

ABGB	Allgemeines bürgerliches Gesetzbuch [Austrian General Civil Code]
ADHGB	Allgemeines deutsches Handelsgesetzbuch [General German Commercial Code]
AHGB	Allgemeines Handelsgesetzbuch [Austrian General Commercial Code]
1850 CL	Ottoman Commercial Law of 1850
1898 CL	Bulgarian Commercial Law of 1898
CPL	Ottoman Commercial Procedure Law
SCC	Serbian Civil Code
SCL	Supplement of the Ottoman Commercial Law

Martin Löhnig, Ivelina Masheva

Introduction

1. The Southeastern European Tectonic Boundary

In the 19th century, the Ottoman Empire, threatened by aggressive foreign powers and internal separatist movements alike, embarked on a mission of sweeping national transformation. This reform era, called the "Tanzimat" (the "Reorganization" in English), started in 1839 with Abdülmecid I's Edict of Gülhane and ended with the advent of the First Constitutional Era in 1876. The program of modernization pursued during the Tanzimat touched a vast array of spheres of Ottoman life; central among them was the legal and judicial system, which was heavily reformed during the period.[1]

Until the Tanzimat period, the Ottoman legal system, especially its commercial law, was predominantly based on Islamic legal traditions; for instance, empirical research has shown that Ottoman company law heavily utilised Islamic legal norms between the 16th–18th centuries. Moreover, court records reveal that Ottoman judges had a uniform legal practice, consistent with that of the medieval Islamic world.[2] In other areas, particularly the treatment of interest, Ottoman jurisprudence gave rise to ingenious legal innovations by adapting medieval Shari'a law to the economic realities of the early modern period. Before the 19th century therefore, the official commercial legal framework in Southeastern Europe was primarily based on Islamic law and displayed a high degree of consistency and uniformity.

During the 19th century however, the homogeneity of this legal and judicial system was increasingly challenged by other legal traditions and ideas, originating both within and without the Empire. The increasing demand for alternative legal solutions itself fueled an increase in the popularity of foreign legal concepts. Accounts of the Tanzimat usually paint the course of the commercial law reforms as a straightforward series of legal acts – the establishment of commercial courts in 1840, the Commercial Law of 1850, the 1860 Appendix to the Commercial Law,

---

1 *Findley, Carter Vaughn*: The Tanzimat, in: Kasaba, Reşat (ed.): Cambridge History of Turkey vol. 4 Turkey in the Modern World, Cambridge and New York 2006, pp. 11–34; *Davison, Roderic*: Reform in the Ottoman Empire 1856–1876, Princeton 1963.

2 *Gerber, Haim*: The Muslim Law of Partnerships in Ottoman Court Records, Studia Islamica, vol. 53 (1981), pp. 109–119; *Çizakça, Murat*: Comparative Evolution of Business Partnerships. The Islamic World and Europe, with Specific Reference to the Ottoman Archives, Leiden 1996; *Gedikli, Fethi*: Osmanlı Şirket Kültürü. XVI.–XVII. Yüzyıllarda Mudarebe Uygulaması, Istanbul 1998.

the 1861 Commercial Procedure Law and the 1863 Law on Maritime Commerce – but this was not, in fact, the case.

The adoption of the new laws has traditionally been interpreted through the dichotomies of modern versus traditional and secular versus religious law. Recent scholarship has, however, started to question this narrative by looking behind the enacted statutory norms and has instead sought to explore the rich legal and judicial practice that existed in the Empire. This approach has allowed for a more nuanced, complex and detailed picture of the evolution of the legal frameworks of 19th and early 20th century Southeastern Europe to be painted, one that emphasizes the consciously syncretic and pluralistic Ottoman law and gives ample expression not only to change and evolution, but to historical continuity as well.[3] By focusing on several clusters of issues and going well beyond a simple analysis of the normative texts, the current volume aims to place commercial law reforms in a larger context. In the Southeastern of Europe, we argue, an independent legal culture developed through a process of the amalgamation of traditional Ottoman legal norms and judicial concepts with 'modern' Western law. The application of the laws was further complicated by a myriad of factors, such as power struggles between different social groups, both within and outside of the government; foreign interference and diplomatic pressures; the existence of special privileged Ottoman merchant classes; and the government's struggle to actually enforce the formal legal equality which existed for non-Muslims.

The internecine power struggles between various factions of the Ottoman elite, combined with the need for separatist movements to be suppressed and the maintenance of imperial power and prestige on the international stage complicated the enactment of law reforms. Although commercial law reforms of the period were primarily aimed at addressing foreign and domestic criticism regarding the perceived deficiencies of Islamic commercial law, they also sought to resolve problems concerning the legal status of non-Muslim minorities and at limiting foreign encroachments on Ottoman sovereignty through the capitulation system.

Capitulations gave foreign merchants operating in Ottoman Empire special legal treatment. In cases not involving an Ottoman subject, for example, foreign merchants had a right of extra-territorial privilege, according to which they could settle their disputes before a consular court. Although mixed cases between Ottomans and foreigners had to be settled in an Ottoman court, foreign merchants had the right to transfer cases worth over a certain sum to Istanbul, the right of *dragoman*,[4]

---

3 *Rubin, Avi*: Ottoman Nizamiye Courts: Law and Modernity, New York 2011; *Rubin, Avi*: Ottoman Judicial Change in the Age of Modernity: A Reappraisal, History Compass, vol. 7 (2009), pp. 119–140.

4 Dragoman literally means translator but it was considered an important privilege because 1. It meant the embassy/consulate needed to be informed about the litigation; 2. Many dragomans had vast experience in commercial trials and served a function similar to modern lawyers.

and the right to dismiss claims based solely on oral testimonies rather than on written documents.[5] In the 18th century and particularly in the 19th century the increased volume of trade with the West and the decline of Ottoman military and political power made capitulation privileges increasingly important with regard to commercial legal litigations.

The complexities of the relationship between the Empire and its ethnic minorities was another theme which affected the development of commercial law in 19th and early 20th century Southeastern Europe. For example, in the Ottoman Empire, non-Muslim subjects had the right to settle their intra-communal disputes in their own judicial institutions under the *millet* system. Additionally, during the 18th and 19th century some non-Muslims Ottoman subjects acquired the special legal status of 'foreign *protégé*' or the special status of a *Avrupa tüccarı* privileged merchant. Moreover, discriminatory practices, such as the unequal treatment of Muslim and non-Muslim testimonies were cited by foreign powers as examples of a failure of the Empire to reform, providing additional impetus to switch to written, formalized judicial procedures.

The course of the commercial law reforms was also heavily dependent on the balance of power between different factions within the Ottoman ruling elite and the Empire's society at large. The first attempt to adopt the French *Code de commerce* in the Ottoman Empire, for example, was made in 1841 by a reformist faction lead by Mustafa Reshid Pasha. However, the attempt faced opposition from conservatives and the religious establishment and failed, causing Mustafa Reshid Pasha's dismissal from the government in the process. A shift in power towards the reformists resulted in the successful adoption of western commercial legal norms in the 1850s and early 1860s. When the possibility of further reform was raised in the late 1860s, the wishes of the conservative faction prevailed and the French *Code civil* was rejected in favour of the maintenance of Islamic law.[6] The ensuing combination and co-existence of secular and religious law, legal transplants and unique, domestically-developed legal traditions, resulted in a complex, heterogeneous and sometimes self-contradictory legal system. This, in turn, created a framework in which legal pluralism and forum shopping could exist, both of which were readily exploited by foreigners and Ottoman subjects.

Finally, in the period under examination, commercial law in Southeastern Europe became increasingly fragmented and varied due to development related to the so-called "Eastern Question". Since the beginning of the 19th century, the Ottoman

5 *Boogert, Maurits van den*: The Capitulations and the Ottoman Legal System Qadis, Consuls and Beratlıs in the 18th Century, Leiden 2005.

6 *Новичев, Арон*: История Турции, vol. 3, part 2, Новое Время (1839–1853), Leningrad 1973, p. 128; *Дюмон, Пол*: Периодът на реформите (Танзимат) (1839–1878), in: Мантран, Робер (ed.): История на Османската империя, Sofia 1999, pp. 489–490.

Empire had suffered a series of territorial losses brought about by the activities of strong non-Muslim minority national separatist movements in the Balkans, combined with the diplomatic and military interventions of foreign powers: Greece attained independence in 1830; Serbia was granted limited autonomy in 1815, followed by full autonomy in 1830; and in 1878 the Treaty of Berlin led to Serbian independence, placed Bosnia and Herzegovina under Austrian rule and established the autonomous Principality of Bulgaria. Thereafter followed Bulgarian independence and Austria-Hungary's annexation of Bosnia and Herzegovina in 1908 and the loss of Albania, Thessaly, Epirus, Macedonia and part of Thrace in 1912. In each of these cases, sovereignty change was followed by nation- and state-building processes which were heavily associated with de-Ottomanization and westernization. Thus, legal and judicial reforms were often aimed at eliminating Ottoman traditions, doctrines and influences, in an effort to 'catch-up' with more developed European states by emulating their legal, judicial, administrative and socio-economic models.

2. Southeastern European legal culture

Taking all these complicating factors into account, this compendium seeks to explore Southeastern European legal culture through the lens of commercial law. It is an area in which the heterogenous nature of the Ottoman legal system, which combined Western legal concepts and indigenous Islamic law, can be easily seen, e.g. through the integration of the mid-19th century French *Code de Commerce*. Newly established or annexed territories often continued to apply Ottoman commercial law for a period of time after the end of Ottoman rule (up to two decades in the case of Bulgaria), albeit in radically altered legal, administrative and economic circumstances. Later in the period, the dominance of French law came to be challenged by the increasing popularity of other European legal systems. German, Austrian and Hungarian law (namely the *Allgemeines Deutsches Handelsgesetzbuch* of 1861 and the *Ungarisches Handelsgesetz* of 1875 which drew much of its content from the former) were particularly influential, as did other European legal codes, such as the 1882 Italian *Codice di Commercio.*

Our hypothesis is, therefore, that Southeastern Europe was located on the 'tectonic boundary' of multiple legal continental shelves during 19th and early 20th century. This position resulted in what we call the 'laboratory of Southeastern Europe', in which elements of different legal cultures existed next to each other, influenced each other or melted together; a legal area characterized by heterogeneity and plurality that appears to be more modern in nature than the classically understood homogenous legal jurisdictions which exercised control over their own continental shelves. This can be illustrated by briefly considering the new commercial codes which developed during the period.

The Greek translation of the first three books of the *Code de Commerce* was enacted as the first Greek commercial code by royal decree on 19 April 1835. Its application was gradually extended to all the territories that were gained in the following decades. This commercial code, originally envisaged as a temporary measure at the beginning of Prince Otto of Bavaria's reign as King of Greece, is still in force today, albeit with numerous alterations. Lacunae in the commercial code were filled through the application, not of the *Code Civil*, but with Greek civil law, i.e. norms shaped by the Roman and Byzantine legal traditions, which were recognized as valid law[7] in the new Greek state in 1835.[8]

The Serbian commercial code of 1860 also recreated the *Code de Commerce* and was supplemented with a law on the bills of exchange based on the German legal tradition, with a separate law on bankruptcy proceedings being enacted the following year. In 1896, a separate stock corporation act, also based on the German model, came into force.[9] In 1905, a commission was appointed to design a new commercial code based on German law. The commission did not succeed in its task however (and neither did future attempts to enact new commercial codes, such as the Yugoslav commercial code which never entered into force after its enactment in 1937), so the 1860 code remained in force until 1946.[10] In 1910, the territorial scope of the code widened considerably, following its almost unconditional adoption in the newly created Kingdom of Montenegro.[11] Complementary regulation concerned with the regulation of other areas of commercial and corporate law existed in the Serbian civil code of 1844, which mirrored the Austrian *Allgemeines Bürgerliches Gesetzbuch*, although it was modified by Serbian customary norms.[12] Accordingly, the civil and commercial codes did not exist in harmony with each other.[13]

Until 1878, Bosna and Herzegovina existed as the Ottoman Province of Bosna and it was not exempted from applying the same laws as the rest of the Empire. When

7 In the Ionian Islands, the Italian-language Civil Code, which came into force in 1841, continued to apply; the Civil Codes of Samos (1899) and Crete (1903) should also be noted, cf. *Plagianakos, Georgios J.*: Die Entstehung des Griechischen Zivilgesetzbuches, Hamburg 1963, p. 41 ss.

8 Cf. *v. Streit, Georg/Diobouniotis, Georg*: Die Griechische Handelsgesetzgebung, in: Dove, Heinrich/ Kohler, Josef/Meyer, Felix/ Trumpler, Hans (eds.): Die Handelsgesetze des Erdballs, 3. Auflage, Band VIII: Süd-Europa II, Teil Griechenland, Berlin 1906, p. 5 s.

9 *Krešić, Mirela/Pastović, Dunja*: Königreich Jugoslawien (1918–1941), in: Löhnig, Martin/Wagner, Stephan (eds.): Das ADHGB von 1861 als gemeinsames Obligationenrecht in Mitteleuropa, Tübingen 2019, p. 228.

10 Ibid., pp. 224, 257.

11 Ibid., p. 251.

12 Cf. *Georgewitsch, Andreas/Michajlowitsch, Stanoje*: Das Handels-, Wechsel- und Konkursrecht Serbiens, in: Dove, Heinrich/Kohler, Josef/Meyer, Felix/Trumpler, Hans (eds.): Die Handelsgesetze des Erdballs, 3. Auflage, Band VIII: Süd-Europa II, Teil Serbien, Berlin 1906, p. 7 s.

13 *Krešić, Mirela/Pastović, Dunja*: op. cit., p. 233.

Austria-Hungary assumed administrative control over Bosnia-Herzegovina in 1878, the courts were instructed to maintain the application of legislation currently in force in their administration of justice and to fill possible gaps by applying Austrian-Hungarian law. By 1883 the Ottoman legislation on trade was replaced by a new commercial code,[14] which was based on the Austrian *AHGB* and the Hungarian commercial code. According to contemporary assessment, the commercial code of 1883 showed progress in the development of commercial law in the province, insofar as foreign norms had been taken into account, from which the province would benefit.[15]

In Romania, a new commercial code came into force in 1887. Although closely based on the Italian commercial code of 1882, the Romanian code drew influences from the commercial legal corpora of Switzerland, Belgium and Germany and further deviated from its original Italian model due to amendments passed soon after its enactment. Moreover, quickly included amendments brought a further deviation from the Italian role model.[16] However, Bukovina, as part of the Habsburg monarchy, applied the Austrian commercial code of 1861, meaning that the norms of the *ADHGB* and Austrian *AHGB* developed during the time of the *Deutscher Bund* were in force in the region. In Transylvania, the Hungarian commercial code of 1875 was applied.[17] A unified commercial code for all Romania did not come into force until 1939. Until that time, the provisions of the general civil law were used to supplement Romania's various commercial codes, i.e. the code of 1887, Bukovina's Austro-Germanic code and Translyvania's Hungarian code.[18]

Ottoman Commercial Code based on the French *Code de commerce* continued to be in force in the Principality of Bulgaria in the first decades following its establishment. Regarding the Bulgarian commercial code of 1898, which replaced the Ottoman legislation, contemporaries noted that, that its editors had utilised

---

14 Sammlung der Gesetze und Verordnungen für Bosnien und die Hercegovina, Sarajevo 1883, Nr. 118, p. 308 ss.

15 *Gertscher, Adalbert*: Das Handels-, Wechsel-, Konkurs- und Seerecht Von Österreich und dem Okkupationsgebiet Bosnien-Herzegowina, in: Dove, Heinrich/Kohler, Josef/Meyer, Felix/Trumpler, Hans (eds.): Die Handelsgesetze des Erdballs, 3. Auflage, Band XIII: Mitteleuropa II, Berlin 1906, p. 302.

16 Cf. *Dimitriu, Vasile/Gane, Stefan G./Flaischlen, Georg*: Das Handels-, Wechsel-, Konkurs- und Seerecht Rumäniens, in: Dove, Heinrich/Kohler, Josef/Meyer, Felix/Trumpler, Hans (eds.): Die Handelsgesetze des Erdballs, 3. Auflage, Band VII: Süd-Europa I, Teil Rumänien, Berlin 1906, p. 2.

17 *Alunaru, Christian*: Königreich Rumänien (1881–1947), in: Löhnig, Martin/Wagner, Stephan (eds.): Das ADHGB von 1861 als gemeinsames Obligationenrecht in Mitteleuropa, Tübingen 2019, p. 291.

18 *Alunaru, Christian*: Ein nichtgeborenes Kind des rumänischen Zivilrechts in der Zwischenkriegszeit: Der Zivilgesetzbuchsentwurf Königs Karl II, in: Löhnig, Martin/Wagner, Stephan (eds.): "Nichtgeborene Kinder des Liberalismus"? Zivilgesetzgebung im Mitteleuropa der Zwischenkriegszeit, Tübingen 2018, p. 224.

Hungarian law (thereby indirectly using German law) to regulate commercial legal transactions and bills of exchange, as well as Romanian law in parts, concerning, for example, the role of women in commerce. For bankruptcy law, the code's editors had clearly used the Romanian commercial code's provisions. Moreover, the contemporary commentators identified the German and Italian commercial codes as providing running sources of inspiration for Bulgaria's new commercial law.[19]

3. Questions Addressed to the Laboratory for Commercial Law in Southeastern Europe

This analysis of the legal culture in Southeastern European will be persued using several methods. First of all, the legal standards of the selected time-frame will be analyzed: how did the legal systems of the respective territories and states change, especially the norms concerning commercial and corporate law, as reflected in their constitutional transformations? When and under what circumstances did the reception or transfer of which commercial and corporate legal norms into the respective legal systems occur? Did this lead to the development of a homogenous legal system or to a state of legal pluralism and how, if such pluralistic states did exist, did the different bodies of norms interact with each other?

However, the exploration of the jurisdictions of Southeastern Europe will go beyond a mere exploration of the history of legal norms; the institutions of those jurisdictions shall also be given considerations. Which authorities or courts dealt with the application of the norms? Which hierarchy or appellate structures existed? Did institutions with overlapping jurisdictions, applying differing norms, coexist easily? How did such institutions recruit their personnel, how were they trained and paid, and to what rules were such personnel subject? What rules existed to guarantee the independence of the judiciary? Which norms governed their judgments and the enforcement thereof? Who represented the parties in court and did a professional class of lawyers ever exist?

Furthermore, with the foundation and international recognition of new nation states in the Balkans during the period, questions of new national jurisprudence arise. Which educational courses could be attended by whom and at which institutions? What textbooks were written and by whom? What legal, cultural and ethnic backgrounds did the authors of such texts have? What kinds of scientific or jurisprudential publications developed? Which foreign works were used and/or

19 Cf. *Schischmanow, Milan St./Subow, Peter A.*: Das Handels-, Wechsel-, Konkurs- und Seerecht Bulgariens, in: Dove, Heinrich/Kohler, Josef/Meyer, Felix/Trumpler, Hans (eds.): Die Handelsgesetze des Erdballs, 3. Auflage, Band VIII: Süd-Europa II, Teil Bulgarien, Berlin 1906, p. 4.

translated in the development of new national jurisprudence? To what extent were aids, such as instructions, commentaries, law reports etc., utilised by courts in their decision-making?

Based on these findings, the practices of courts in Southeastern Europe will be analysed. What insights can be gained from a quantitative analysis of data, such as the number of proceedings conducted before courts, the personal characteristics of the parties, the issues being litigated, the availability and usage of ordinary and extrajudicial legal remedies, and the necessity for judicial enforcement of decisions? What can be learned from a qualitative analysis of the styles of judgment and utilisation of legal norms from individual judgments? Are there discrepancies between the black-letter law and the law as practised in court and what role, if any, did custom or tradition play in influencing proceedings? How did the parties undertake their submissions and to which authorities did they refer? How were court proceedings undertaken? Is there any evidence that courts were affected by bribery, patronage or other illegitimate influences? How and when did the courts order their judgments enforced and how effectively were such orders carried out?

This book contains three studies on commercial law in Southeastern Europe: Mehmed Bećić examines commercial disputes and the application of Ottoman commercial law in Bosnia and Herzegovina in the early post-Ottoman period. Ivelina Masheva shows that there was a significant degree of continuity in commercial law during the period spanning the last decades of Ottoman rule and first decades of independence in the Principality of Bulgaria (1840s–1890s). Zoran S. Mirković examines commercial law and commercial disputes in Serbia between 1840–1860.

Mehmed Bećić

Commercial Disputes and Application of Ottoman Commercial Law in Bosnia and Herzegovina

1. Introduction

The Ottoman province of Vilayet Bosna was occupied by Austria-Hungary in 1878, which, for the following four decades, would govern the region. The occupied province, officially renamed Bosnia and Herzegovina, became in fact a separate administrative-territorial unit *(corpus separatum)* of Austria-Hungary. It was administered by the Joint Austro-Hungarian Government through the Provincial Government for Bosnia and Herzegovina in Sarajevo. The occupation in 1878 marked a turning point in Bosnia's political, social, economic, cultural, and legal history. The changes brought the province closer to new European trends in many areas, while also retaining domestic, Islamic, and local elements and traditions.

In that sense, the new administration left many Ottoman institutions and laws in force, in order to gradually change them by legal transplantation (reception) of laws originating from the legal systems of Austria-Hungary. Thus, the Ottoman commercial legislation of the Tanzimat era was replaced as late as 1883, when new commercial legislation for Bosnia and Herzegovina was adopted. This means that Ottoman commercial law was formally valid during the first five years of Austro-Hungarian rule in Bosnia and Herzegovina.

The aim of this paper is to reconstruct commercial disputes and investigate the application of Ottoman commercial law in Bosnia and Herzegovina in the early post-Ottoman period, i.e., in the time before the adoption of the Commercial Law for Bosnia and Herzegovina (1878–1883). The main research questions of this paper are as follows: which judicial institutions were competent to resolve commercial disputes, who were the judges of those courts, what was the applied substantive law in commercial cases, what documents and evidence were used by the parties and what was the role of Ottoman commercial law in court proceedings.

Modern legal and historical literature did not deal with the development of commercial law in Bosnia and Herzegovina in the second half of the 19th century. However, historical research on development of cities, economy and society of that time has a long tradition in the historical science of Bosnia and Herzegovina.[1] This

1 For Example: *Hauptmann, Ferdo*: Privreda i društvo Bosne i Hercegovine u doba austrougarske vladavine (1878–1918), Prilozi za istoriju Bosne i Hercegovine, II, Akademija nauka i umjetnosti Bosne

historical research has continued in modern literature. As a result, two studies on trade relations in Bosnia from the second half of the 19th century were recently published, one dealing with trade policy in Bosnia and Herzegovina during the Austro-Hungarian rule, and the other with trade relations and trade elites in Bosnia in the late Ottoman period.[2] However, the analysis of commercial law and the practice of commercial courts in the late Ottoman and Austro-Hungarian period were completely absent in modern literature. Only recently have first steps been taken in this direction.[3]

Having in mind the absence of literary sources, this paper is based mainly on archival and normative sources. Archival sources include court documents: judgments, lawsuits and various other documents from late Ottoman and early Austro-Hungarian period.[4] In addition to archival documents, the work relies on various normative sources. Among the most important is the Collection of Laws, Orders and Norms Issued for Bosnia and Herzegovina from 1881 *(Sammlung der für Bosnien und die Hercegovina erlassenen Gesetze, Verordnungen und Normalweisungen)*.[5] Other important sources are: the Books of Decisions in Civil Matters of the Supreme Court for Bosnia and Herzegovina *(Präjudicienbücher in Civilsachen)*[6] and various newspaper sources from late Ottoman and early post-Ottoman times, report letters etc.

The paper is divided into four parts. The first part analyzes the reform of the commercial courts in Bosnia and Herzegovina and the process of reviving Ottoman commercial legislation after 1878. The second part provides a brief description of commercial disputes before regular courts. It describes the parties, the content of typical commercial disputes and the evidence used in these proceedings. The third part of the paper analyzes the sources of substantive law applied in commercial

---

i Hercegovine, Posebna izdanja, Knjiga LXXIX, Odjeljenje društvenih nauka, Knjiga 18, Sarajevo 1987; *Juzbašić, Dževad* (ed.): Politika i privreda u Bosni i Hercegovini pod austrougarskom upravom, Akademija nauka i umjetnosti Bosne i Hercegovine, Posebna izdanja, Knjiga CXVI, Odjeljenje društvenih nauka, Knjiga 35, Sarajevo 2002.

2 *Kasumović, Amila*: Austrougarska trgovinska politika u Bosni i Hercegovini 1878–1914, Sarajevo 2016 and *Younis, Hana*: Od dućana do pozorišta – sarajevska trgovačka elita 1851–1878, Sarajevo 2017.

3 In 2020, I mentored a master's thesis on the establishment and organization of commercial courts in late Ottoman Bosnia (during the Tanzimat period).

4 Mainly from the Archives of Bosnia and Herzegovina, Supreme Court for Bosnia and Herzegovina – Sarajevo (Arhiv Bosne i Hercegovine, Vrhovni sud za Bosnu i Hercegovinu – Sarajevo; hereinafter: ABH, VSS).

5 Sammlung der für Bosnien und die Hercegovina erlassenen Gesetze, Verordnungen und Normalweisungen, 1878–1880, II. Band, Justizverwaltung, Wien 1881.

6 Präjudicienbuch in Civilsachen, Obergericht für Bosnien und die Hercegovina, Sarajevo.

disputes. Finally, the fourth part analyzes the application of certain rules of Ottoman commercial law in the practice of regular courts.

2. Reorganization of commercial courts and translation of Ottoman commercial legislation

Immediately after the occupation in 1878, the new Austro-Hungarian administration began restoring and reorganizing the judicial organization in Bosnia and Herzegovina. In essence, the Ottoman judicial structure of the Tanzimat period was retained. This was already made clear with the first orders on the organization of courts.[7] Regular/secular *(nizamiye)* and Sharia courts as state-courts and ecclesiastical courts as non-state courts continued their judicial function. The jurisdiction of the consular courts for foreigners was also temporarily retained. But with these orders, the new administration introduced some important changes in the organization of the judiciary.[8]

The most important of these interventions were: 1. introduction of a two-instance judiciary with the newly established Supreme Court for Bosnia and Herzegovina at the top (as a court of second and last instance);[9] 2. the abolition of the lay element from the judiciary; 3. the abolition of commercial courts and transfer of jurisdiction over commercial cases to regular courts; and 4. the appointment of judicial officers from Austria-Hungary to all judicial positions in the regular courts.[10] In parallel with this process, the Ottoman laws were translated into German – they remained in force until they were replaced by new laws (legal transplants from Austria-Hungary). The following is a brief overview of these activities of the new administration.

---

7 Sammlung der für Bosnien und die Hercegovina erlassenen Gesetze, Verordnungen und Normalweisungen, 1878–1880, II. Band, Justizverwaltung, pp. 3–15 (This collection is hereinafter referred to as "Band II, Justizverwaltung"); *Sladović, Eugen*: Priručnik zakona i naredaba za upravnu službu u Bosni i Hercegovini, Sarajevo 1915, p. 310.

8 Circularerlass der Landesregierung in Sarajevo vom 30. December 1878., Nr. 436 Just., betreffend die Organisation der Gerichte – Beilage (Band II, Justizverwaltung, p. 5); *Bećić, Mehmed*: Das Privatrecht in Bosnien-Herzegowina (1878–1918): Zur Koexistenz österreichischer und ottomanischer Rechtsinstitutionen, in: Thomas Simon (ed.): Konflikt und Koexistenz – Die Rechtsordnungen Südosteuropas im 19. und 20. Jahrhundert, Band II, Serbien, Bosnien-Herzegowina, Albanien, Frankfurt am Main 2017, pp. 72–87.

9 See: Verordnung der Landesregierung in Sarajevo vom 6. Juli 1879., Nr. 11287, Just. 2011, betreffend die Constituirung des Obergerichtes (Band II, Justizverwaltung, p. 21) und Verordnung der Landesregierung in Sarajevo vom 17. Juli 1879., Nr. 1390 Präs., betreffend die Instruction für das Obergericht in Sarajevo (Band II, Justizverwaltung, p. 22).

10 Circularerlass der Landesregierung in Sarajevo vom 30. December 1878., Nr. 436 Just., betreffend die Organisation der Gerichte – Beilage (Band II, Justizverwaltung, p. 5); *Bećić, Mehmed*: Das Privatrecht in Bosnien-Herzegowina (1878–1918), pp. 79–82.

2.1 Reorganization of commercial courts

During the Tanzimat period, special commercial courts were introduced throughout the Ottoman Empire.[11] The function of these courts was to deal with commercial cases in accordance with the new commercial legislation (based on French law). In Vilayet Bosna, as an Ottoman province, the Ottoman government managed to establish such commercial courts only in three cities: Sarajevo, Mostar and Banja Luka.[12] The courts had a lay character and were composed of a presiding judge and two permanent and four changing members (assessors) who were elected from the merchant class.[13] The Supreme Commercial Court in Constantinople was to be established as a second instance. However, by the time of the occupation in 1878, this court had not been established. So, appeals in commercial cases had to be resolved by the commercial court at the seat of the Vilayet Bosna (Sarajevo) or the Supreme Court in Constantinople.[14]

There are no published studies in the recent literature about the commercial courts in Bosnia of the late Ottoman period. However, by looking at archival and other sources, it can be concluded that these courts were functioning during the last decade of the Ottoman administration in Bosnia. It seems that domestic merchants were at first reluctant to settle their disputes before these courts.[15] This changed gradually from the late 1860s until the occupation of Bosnia in 1878. By inspecting some unpublished archival materials, it can be concluded that during the 1870s, domestic merchants resolved their disputes regularly before the commercial courts.[16] In addition, from official vilayet press during the 1860s and 1870s, we can see that bankruptcy proceedings of domestic merchants were conducted by commercial courts in the Vilayet.[17] From the same sources we learn that these courts acted in accordance with the new Ottoman commercial laws. Thus, despite

11 *Aličić, Ahmed S.*: Uređenje Bosanskog ejaleta od 1789. do 1878. godine, Sarajevo 1983, pp. 135–140.

12 *Eichler, Eduard*: Das Justizwesen Bosniens und der Hercegovina, Landesregierung für Bosnien und die Hercegovina, Wien 1889, p. 59.

13 See: *Eichler, Eduard*: op. cit., p. 59; *Aličić, Ahmed S.*: op. cit., pp. 135–139.

14 *Eichler, Eduard*: op. cit., p. 59; *Schmid, Ferdinand*: Bosnien und die Herzegovina unter der Verwaltung Österreich-Ungarns, Leipzig 1914, pp. 117–118.

15 Such an impression was gained by Ahmet Dževdet – pasha who was in Bosnia as an judicial inspector (*mufetish*) for the Ottoman government in 1864. See: *Kreševjaković, Hamdija*: Iz bosanske trgovine XIX stoljeća, Narodna starina, vol. 1 (1922), no. 2, pp. 162–164; *Kreševjaković, Hamdija*: Dževdet-pašina pisma o Bosni iz 1864. godine, Sarajevo 1932.

16 Conclusion based on insight into archival sources in the form of decisions of the Commercial Court in Sarajevo in the late Ottoman period (sources from the Archives of BiH).

17 *Kreševjaković, Hamdija*: Stečajevi u Bosni 1867–1877, Narodna Starina, vol. 13 (1934), no. 34, pp. 189–192. For Example: "Bosna" (Nr. 416 from 30 Rebiulahira 1291 – 3 (15) June 1874; Nr. 495 od 21 Zilkade 1292 – 8 (20) December 1875).

the difficult implementation of the new courts during the Tanzimat period, the organization of the Ottoman commercial courts in Bosnia did not remain a dead letter. The law in action perspective indicates that the Ottoman commercial courts in Bosnia functioned and applied the new Ottoman commercial law.

After the Austro-Hungarian occupation of the Vilayet Bosnia, the Ottoman commercial courts were abolished. Already in the first orders on the organization of courts it was ordered that special commercial courts were to be abolished and that commercial cases were to be transferred under the jurisdiction of regular courts, i.e. county courts. In the Circular order regarding the organization of the courts of 30 December 1878 *(Cirkularerlass der Landesregierung in Sarajevo vom 30. December 1878., betreffend die Organisation der Gerichte)* it was prescribed:

> "The courts existing according to the previous regulations, namely the county courts in the county capitals (medžlissi temjizi) and the district courts at the headquarters of the capitals of the districts (medžlissi daavi) will continue with their functions. Regardless of whether or not a commercial court (tidžaret mehkemissi) was systemized in the district, the county courts also have to deal exclusively with commercial court agendas for the entire territorial extent of the county."[18]

However, the organization of the judiciary had a provisional character during the first months and years of the new administration.[19] During that time, the judiciary faced a number of problems, one of which was the lack of a civil procedure law and clear division of jurisdiction between individual courts. Therefore, it should come as no surprise that during the first years of Austro-Hungarian rule, there were overlapping jurisdictions between courts.[20] It is probable that in everyday practice commercial cases also came before lower, regular district courts or sharia courts. This is at least indicated by special instructions of the government, in which it is repeatedly emphasized that commercial disputes fall within the jurisdiction of the county courts *(Kreisgericht; Okružni sud)*.[21] The precise division of jurisdiction

---

18 Band II, Justizverwaltung, p. 4: „Die nach den bisherigen Vorschriften bestehenden Gerichte und zwar die Kreisgerichte an den Kreisorten (medžlissi temjizi) und die Bezirksgerichte am Sitze der Hauptorte der Bezirke (medžlissi daavi) haben bis auf Weiteres ihre Functionen fortzusetzen. Die Kreisgerichte haben jedoch ohne Rücksicht darauf, ob in dem Kreisorte ein Handelsgericht (tidžaret mehkemissi) systemisiert war oder nicht, auch die handelsgerichtlichen Agenden für den ganzen territorialen Umfang des Kreises ausschließlich zu besorgen."

19 For a detailed overview, see: *Eichler, Eduard*: op. cit., p. 105; *Bećić, Mehmed*: Austrougarska reforma pravosuđa i građanskog postupka u Bosni i Hercegovini, Godišnjak Pravnog fakulteta u Sarajevu, vol. LVIII (2015), p. 111.

20 See: *Eichler, Eduard*: op. cit., pp. 196–200.

21 „Mit der Kundmachung vom 30. December v.J. wurde verlautbart, dass die in den Kreisorten aufgestellten Kreisgerichte zugleich auch Handelsgerichte sind. Eingaben an diese sind daher den

between the courts in civil (and commercial cases) did not occur until 1883, after the enactment of the Law on Civil Procedure for Bosnia and Herzegovina.[22]

The new administration had its reasons for not retaining special commercial courts in Bosnia and Herzegovina. Eduard Eichler, a government official who held the most important judicial functions since the establishment of Austro-Hungarian administration, cites two main reasons for abolishing commercial courts in Bosnia and Herzegovina. The first reason is that the Ottoman administration did not complete the establishment of these courts throughout the country, and the second is the finances – the existence of commercial courts would further burden the budget of the new administration.[23] Apart from these official motives, the very composition of the Ottoman commercial courts, which included domestic merchants, was probably unacceptable for the new administration. Thus, commercial cases were handed over to the jurisdiction of the newly formed regular courts headed by Austro-Hungarian officials. However, the existing Ottoman institution of the *Majlis (Medžlis)* – assessors *(Beisitzer)* was retained in commercial processes,[24] while in all other civil and criminal proceedings they were definitively abolished at the latest after the entry into force of the Instruction for Courts *(Gerichtsinstruction)* in 1881.[25]

The staff of the regular courts, which were given jurisdiction over commercial cases, was a major novelty compared to the Ottoman era. Instead of Ottoman judges and domestic merchants, commercial cases were now decided by judges from Austria-Hungary. This was a consequence of the sudden dismissal of almost all judicial officials in the country after the establishment of the new administration in Bosnia and Herzegovina. With the exception of the Sharia courts, in which the domestic Sharia judges were retained, all other legal positions in administration,

---

Kreisgerichten zu übergeben. Dies wird wiederhold zur Kenntniss gebracht." (Band II, Justizverwaltung, p. 19).

22 For more details, see: *Bećić, Mehmed*: Austrougarska reforma pravosuđa i građanskog postupka u Bosni i Hercegovini, pp. 107–124.

23 *Eichler, Eduard*: op. cit., p. 139.

24 „Bei allen oben erwähnten Gerichtsbehörden wäre die Beiziehung der Laienelemente in der Regel auszuschliessen, und es könnte eine Theilnahme von Laien bei der Rechtssprechung nur in Handels- und Wechselsachen als nützlich bezeichnet werden." (Band II, Justizverwaltung, p. 3).

25 „Das Institut der Gerichtsbeisitzer (Medžlisse) tritt mit dem Tage der Wirksamkeit der Gerichtsinstruction bei allen Kreisgerichten und Bezirksbehörden als Gerichte ausser Kraft, und sind dieselben von diesem Tage angefangen zur Judicatur auch in Civil-Rechtsangelegenheiten nicht mehr heranzuziehen, sondern von den Kreis- und Bezirksgerichten ohne Mitwirkung von Medžlisse zu verhandeln und zu entscheiden ... Hiedurch bleibt das Institut der Handels-Gerichtsbeisitzer unberührt" (Sammlung der Gesetze und Verordnungen für Bosnien und die Hercegovina, Jahrgang 1881, Sarajevo 1881, p. 302).

legislation and justice were filled by officials from Austria-Hungary.[26] This process also included the regular courts that had jurisdiction over commercial matters.

The new composition of the judicial staff also meant the transformation of the so-called internal legal culture – from an Ottoman to a new European/German/Austrian (conditionally into a mixed Ottoman-German) legal culture. The origin, legal training, legal practice and legal style of the new officials in Bosnia and Herzegovina show that they can be described as lawyers of German or Austrian legal culture. As for the origin of the new lawyers, we learn from the archival sources and biographies of the officials that they came from different parts of Austria-Hungary. Still, the administration preferred officials of Slavic origin from Croatia, Slavonia, Dalmatia and other Slavic language areas, due to the similarity of the languages.[27] With regard to the educational profile, there was a uniform picture among the new judicial officers: after graduating from high school (Gymnasium), they studied law at one of the universities in Austria-Hungary (Vienna, Zagreb, Prague, Budapest, Graz, etc.).[28] They completed their law studies according to the reformed study program (Thun-Hohenstein University Reform),[29] which at that time was influenced by the German historical school of law and pandect school.[30] The legal practice and the legal style of the new lawyers also indicate that they belong to the German/Austrian legal culture – this is clearly evidenced by the style and content of the court decisions and their rationale.

One of the problems in the functioning of the judiciary of Bosnia and Herzegovina during the first years of the new Austro-Hungarian administration was precisely the new court officials in the lowest, district courts *(Bezirksgericht)*. Namely, the trial function was performed mainly by young and unexperienced auscultants (trainees) and adjuncts.[31] They obviously could not meet the challenge of resolving complex

26 *Bećić, Mehmed*: Das Privatrecht in Bosnien-Herzegowina (1878–1918), pp. 82–87.

27 Ibid., p. 86.

28 Ibid., pp. 85–87.

29 For a detailed overview, see: *Simon, Thomas*: Thun-Hohensteinsche Universitätsreform und die Neuordnung der juristischen Studien- und Prüfungsordnung in Österreich, in: Zoran Pokrovac (ed.): Juristenausbildung in Osteuropa bis zum Ersten Weltkrieg, Rechtskulturen des modernen Osteuropa. Traditionen und Transfers, Band 3, Frankfurt am Main 2007, pp. 1–36.

30 See: *Ebert, Kurt*: Die Pflege der Rechtsgeschichte an der Universität Graz im Zeichen der Historischen Schule, Zeitschrift der Savigny-Stiftung für Rechtsgeschichte, Germanistische Abteilung, vol. 87 (1970), p. 242; *Čepula, Dalibor*: Legal education in Croatia from medieval times to 1918: Institutions, courses of study and transfers, in: Zoran Pokrovac (ed.): Juristenausbildung in Osteuropa bis zum Ersten Weltkrieg, Rechtskulturen des modernen Osteuropa. Traditionen und Transfers, Band 3, Frankfurt am Main 2007, p. 128.

31 Band II, Justizverwaltung, pp. 16–18; *Eichler, Eduard*: op. cit., p. 145; „Anlässlich, einer vorgekommenen Anfrage über den Wirkungskreis und die amtliche Stellung der bei den Bezirksbehörden angestellten österreichisch-ungarischen Gerichtsbeamten (Adjunct oder Auscultant) diene bis zur Sanctionirung des Statutes über die Einrichtung und Amtswirksamkeit der Bezirksbehörden zur

legal issues in the new circumstances in Bosnia and Herzegovina (occupation, re-establishment of the state and judicial apparatus, unknown domestic law, language barriers, (Latin) illiteracy of a large part of the native population etc.).[32] Unlike the lowest, district courts, older and more experienced lawyers were appointed to the positions of higher courts, i.e. county courts *(Kreisgerichte)* and the newly formed Supreme Court for Bosnia and Herzegovina *(Obergericht für Bosnien und die Herzegovina)*.[33] In addition, in these higher courts, decisions were made by judicial councils (senates). All this ensured a greater degree of legal certainty, legal knowledge and legal skills in resolving commercial cases, for which the county courts were competent in the first instance, and the Supreme Court in the second instance.

2.2 Continuity of Ottoman commercial legislation in the form of German translations

The new Austro-Hungarian government decided to temporarily maintain the existing Ottoman law in Bosnia and Herzegovina. The old Ottoman law was to be valid until new laws were imposed for Bosnia and Herzegovina. The exceptions were those laws that were contrary to the general legal principles and interests of the Monarchy. This principle was emphasized in the Provisional Scope of Work of the Head of the Provincial Government *(Provisorischer Wirkungskreis des Chefs der Landesregierung in Bosnien und der Hercegovina)*,[34] and then further elaborated in special orders and instructions on the organization of courts issued in late 1878 and early 1879.[35] From these provisional orders two general principles governing the question of the continuity and discontinuity of domestic (Ottoman) law in

Richtschnur, dass der richterliche Functionär mit Ausnahme der dem Kadi vorbehaltenen Führung der Scheriatsangelegenheiten, sämtliche Gerichtsgeschäfte ganz selbstständig und unter eigener Verantwortung zu versehen und auch die Entscheidungen zu unterschreiben hat." (Circularerlass der Landesregierung in Sarajevo vom 12. März 1880., Nr. 1203 Just., betreffend den Wirkungskreis der richterlichen Functionäre bei den Bezirksbehörden, Band II, Justizverwaltung, p. 31).

32 *Eichler, Eduard*: op. cit., pp. 191–192.

33 Ibid., p. 145.

34 Sammlung der für Bosnien und die Hercegovina erlassenen Gesetze, Verordnungen und Normalweisungen, I. Band, Allgemeiner Theil, Wien 1880, p. 13 (Provisorischer Wirkungskreis des Chefs der Landesregierung in Bosnien und der Hercegovina-Uebergangsbestimmungen).

35 *Sladović, Eugen*: Priručnik zakona i naredaba za upravnu službu u Bosni i Hercegovini, p. 310; Band II, Justizverwaltung, pp. 3–5 (Circularerlass der Landesregierung in Sarajevo vom 30. December 1878., Nr. 436 Just., betreffend die Organisation der Gerichte); Band II, Justizverwaltung, pp. 5–15 (Erlass des gemeinsamen Ministeriums vom 1. Jänner 1879, Nr. 693 B.H., betreffend die Organisation der Justizverwaltung); Band II, Justizverwaltung, p. 23 (§ 12 Instruction für das Obergericht in Sarajevo vom 17. Juli 1879.)

Bosnia and Herzegovina were derived: first, Ottoman law remains in force until it is replaced by new laws; second, in the case of legal gaps in civil matters, the courts may, by analogy, apply the law in force in Austria-Hungary (in practice this meant the application of the Austrian General Civil Code – ABGB).[36]

In order for this principle to be implemented in practice, the new administration had to determine which laws were in force in Bosnia before the occupation in 1878 and to prepare translations of Ottoman laws into German.[37] Translations were necessary so that the new officials in the judiciary and administration could apply Ottoman laws. A commission was soon set up within the Provincial Government in Sarajevo to investigate the domestic (Ottoman) laws, while the Oriental Academy in Vienna and the Dragoman Department at the Provincial Government were given the task of translating these laws into German.[38] The mentioned commission proposed, and the government adopted a conclusion that only laws published in the official Ottoman Collection of Laws *Düstūr* were accepted as the valid, pre-exisiting law in Bosnia and Herzegovina.[39]

During 1879 and 1880, the Provincial Government translated and republished certain Ottoman laws and regulations from *Düstūr* in the form of special orders.[40] After researching, systematizing and translating the Ottoman legislation from the Tanzimat era, these republished laws and orders, together with numerous other German translations of Ottoman laws, orders and regulations were collected and published in a collection entitled *Collection of Laws, Orders and Norms Issued for*

36 *Bećić, Mehmed*: Das Privatrecht in Bosnien-Herzegowina (1878–1918), p. 99; *Bećić, Mehmed*: Primjena Medželle u postosmanskoj Bosni i Hercegovini, Godišnjak Pravnog fakulteta u Sarajevu, vol. LVII (2014), pp. 51–66; *Bećić, Mehmed*: Osmansko tanzimatsko pravo i austrougarski pravni poredak u Bosni i Hercegovini, Anali Pravnog fakulteta u Zenici, vol. 12 (2013), pp. 187–201; *Bećić, Mehmed*: Historijska i pravna osnovanost primjene Općeg građanskog zakonika u Bosni i Hercegovini nakon okupacije 1878. godine, Godišnjak Pravnog fakulteta u Sarajevu, vol. LIV (2011), pp. 63–79.

37 Band II, Justizverwaltung, p. 8.

38 Archives of Bosnia and Herzegovina, Provincial Government in Sarajevo, 11, 24/19, 1881. (Archiv Bosne i Hercegovine, Zemaljska vlada za Sarajevo, hereinafter: ABH, ZVS); „Im Lande fand sich nicht die ottomanische Staatsgesetzsammlung und kein vollständige Exemplar der in Sarajewo zur Zeit der ottmanischen Regierung bestandenen Amtsblattes. Nach und nach fanden sich wohl einzelne ottomanische Gesetze in slavischer Übersetzung. Ebenso stand die bekannte französische Übersetzung von Aristarchi Bey zur Verfügung. Wären diese Übersetzungen aber auch verläßlicher gewesen, als sie es sind, eine authentische deutsche Übersetzung war unentbehrlich. An dieser authentischen deutschen Übersetzung wurde und wird in anstrengender Weise in Wien bei der orientalischen Akademie und in Serajevo bei dem Dragomanat, einer bei der bosnischen Landesregierung wesentlich zu Übersetzungszwecken bestellten Behörde gearbeitet." (Grazer Volksblatt, 15. Jahrgang, Nr. 86, Graz, 15 April 1882, p. 5).

39 ABH, ZVS, 11, 24/19, 1881.

40 *Eichler, Eduard*: op. cit. p. 173.

Bosnia and Herzegovina (Sammlung der für Bosnien und die Hercegovina erlassenen Gesetze, Verordnungen und Normalweisungen).[41]

Most of the Ottoman civil legislation was found in the second volume *(Justizverwaltung)* of this collection. It contained Ottoman legislation (in the field of property law and parts of the law of obligations), but also a number of laws that regulated various procedural and organizational issues. Translations of Ottoman commercial legislation (substantive and procedural law) were also published in this volume, namely:

- Commercial Code of 1860 *(Handelsgesetz vom 9. Scheval 1276 (30. April 1860));*[42]
- Appendix to the Commercial Code of 1860 *(Anhang zum Handelsgesetz vom 9. Scheval 1276 (30. April 1860));*[43]
- Law on the Procedure in Commercial Matters *(Gesetz über das Verfahren in Handelssachen, vom 10. Rebiul-ahir 1278);*[44]
- Law on Contracts in Commercial Matters *(Gesetz über Verträge in Handelssachen).*[45]

In 1881, the *Sammlung* (Collection) was distributed to all courts and administrative bodies in Bosnia and Herzegovina.[46] Thus, it was possible for the new officials to get acquainted with the content of the Ottoman state legislation from the Tanzimat period. In this way, the Austro-Hungarian authorities provided the basic legal and technical conditions for the continued validity and application of Ottoman commercial legislation in Bosnia and Herzegovina. These commercial laws remained in force until they were replaced in 1883 by new laws – legal transplants of Austrian/Hungarian/German commercial legislation. This 1883 legal reform was prepared by the so-called Judicial Commission *(Justizkommission)* headed by Alois Lapenna, which assessed that Bosnia and Herzegovina needed new laws on civil procedure, a law on Sharia courts, as well as new commercial, bankruptcy and

41 For a detailed overview, see: *Karčić, Fikret*: Survival of the Ottoman-Islamic Laws in post-Ottoman Times in Bosnia and Herzegovina, in: Thomas Simon (ed.): Konflikt und Koexistenz – Die Rechtsordnungen Südosteuropas im 19. und 20. Jahrhundert, Band II, Serbien, Bosnien-Herzegowina, Albanien, Frankfurt am Main 2017, pp. 43–70.

42 Band II, Justizverwaltung, pp. 395–439.

43 Band II, Justizverwaltung, pp. 439–452.

44 Band II, Justizverwaltung, pp. 453–471.

45 Band II, Justizverwaltung, pp. 471–472.

46 *Eichler, Eduard*: op. cit., p. 174.

bill of exchange laws.[47] One of the motives for replacing the Ottoman commercial legislation with legal transplants from Austria-Hungary was certainly the facilitated trade between Bosnia and Herzegovina and the rest of the Monarchy. At that time a customs union (single customs area) had already been established between Bosnia and Herzegovina and the rest of the Monarchy, and the unification of commercial law in the entire area facilitated trade, especially its export-import component.

Thus, the Ottoman Commercial Code of 1860 was replaced by a set of new laws – legal transplants of Austrian and Hungarian law – which came into force on 1 November 1883,[48] namely: Bill of Exchange Law for Bosnia and Herzegovina of 12 April 1883 (*Mjenični (Mjenidbeni) zakon* za Bosnu i Hercegovinu),[49] Bankruptcy Order of 26 May 1883 *(Stečajni red)*[50] and the Commercial Law for Bosnia and Herzegovina of 7 June 1883 (*Trgovački zakon).*[51] The Commercial Law for Bosnia and Herzegovina was a legal transplant of the Hungarian Commercial Law of 1875[52] that is Austrian and German commercial law (*Allgemeines deutsches Handelsgesetzbuch* – ADHGB). A comparative analysis of the legal texts confirmed that the Commercial Law for Bosnia and Herzegovina was drafted according to the text of the Hungarian Law, with certain deviations.[53] The legal text of the Bill of Exchange Law for Bosnia and Herzegovina was almost verbatim taken from the Austrian Law of 25 January 1850.[54] This is confirmed by a comparative analysis of legal texts and the bill's original Austrian Law for Bosnia and Herzegovina.[55] There were only minimal deviations from Bill of Exchange Law in the rest of the Monarchy.[56] The Bankruptcy Order for Bosnia and Herzegovina was compiled on the basis of the Hungarian Bankruptcy Order of 1881 and the Austrian Bankruptcy Order of

---

47 *Bećić, Mehmed*: Novi pogled na transformaciju šerijatskih sudova u Bosni i Hercegovini: da li je 1883. godine nametnut kolonijalni model primjene šerijatskog prava?, Godišnjak Pravnog fakulteta u Sarajevu, vol. LX (2017), pp. 67–68.

48 Zbornik zakona i naredaba za Bosnu i Hercegovinu, Godina 1883, Sarajevo 1883, pp. 305, 449.

49 Ibid., pp. 450–476.

50 Ibid., pp. 623–677.

51 Ibid., pp. 308–439.

52 *Eichler, Eduard*: op. cit., p. 262; Izvještaj o upravi BiH 1906, Zagreb 1906, p. 37.

53 Compare: Das ungarische Handelsgesetz. Deutsche Ausgabe, Budapest 1876, pp. 206–232 and Trgovački zakon za Bosnu i Hercegovinu, Zbornik zakona i naredaba za Bosnu i Hercegovinu, Godina 1883, pp. 308–439.

54 *Eichler, Eduard*: op. cit., p. 266; Izvještaj o upravi BiH 1906, p. 37; Bosnischer Boote pro 1901. Universal-Hand- und Adressbuch für Bosnien-Hercegovina, Sarajevo 1901, p. 39.

55 Compare: Mjenidbeni zakon za Bosnu i Hercegovinu (Zbornik zakona i naredaba za Bosnu i Hercegovinu, Godina 1883., pp. 450–476) and „Allgemeine Wechselordnung für die k. k. österreichischen Staaten" in: Allgemeines Reichs-Gesetz- und Regierungsblatt für das Kaiserthum Oesterreich, Jahrgang 1850, Erster Theil, Wien 1850, pp. 593–608.

56 Izvještaj o upravi BiH 1906, p. 37; Bosnischer Boote pro 1901, p. 39.

25 December 1868,[57] but here too there were certain deviations and adjustments to the domestic business environment and the legal order.[58]

Formally, the procedural rules of the Ottoman Law on Procedure in Commercial Matters ceased to apply after the enactment of the Civil Procedure for Bosnia and Herzegovina in 1883 (which was also made on the basis an Austrian Draft from 1881).[59] However, even earlier, these procedural rules were supplemented and replaced in court practice by the application of the rules of the Hungarian-Transylvanian civil procedure.[60]

Thus, Ottoman commercial law ceased to be valid at the end of 1883. The exceptions were obviously the statutory provisions for damages (i.e. statutory interest) from the Appendix to the Ottoman Commercial Code of 1860 *(Anhang zum Handelsgesetz vom 9. Scheval 1276 (30. April 1860))*,[61] which continued to be valid. In line with this development, it can be concluded that the Ottoman trade legislation from the Tanzimat period went through three phases in Bosnia and Herzegovina:

- From the 1860s to 1878, it was formally valid and applied in commercial cases, decided by commercial court within the Ottoman administration.
- From 1878 to 1883, it formally continued to be valid and was applied in practice in the form of official German translations. In these years, court practice developed a special form of legal pluralism: judges supplemented and replaced the existing Ottoman law in court practice with the rules of civil substantive (ABGB) and procedural law (Hungarian-Transylvanian civil procedure) known to them.
- After 1 November 1883, Ottoman commercial legislation was no longer in force. It was replaced by new commercial laws in the form of legal transplants of German, Austrian and Hungarian law. In this research, it was found that only certain rules of Ottoman commercial law survived this reform (e.g. rules on damages/statutory interest), which will be discussed later.

---

57 *Eichler, Eduard*: op. cit. p. 268.; Izvještaj o upravi BiH 1906, p. 37; Bosnischer Boote pro 1901, p. 39.

58 Izvještaj o upravi BiH 1906, p. 37; Bosnischer Boote pro 1901, p. 39.

59 See futher: *Bećić, Mehmed*: Austrougarska reforma pravosuđa i građanskog postupka u Bosni i Hercegovini, pp. 107–124.; *Bećić, Mehmed*: Das Privatrecht in Bosnien-Herzegowina (1878–1918), pp. 108–114.

60 See: *Bećić, Mehmed*: Austrougarska reforma pravosuđa i građanskog postupka u Bosni i Hercegovini, pp. 107–124; *Bećić, Mehmed*: Das Privatrecht in Bosnien-Herzegowina (1878–1918), pp. 108–109.

61 Band II, Justizverwaltung, pp. 439–452.

3. A brief look at the courtroom: parties, cases, and documents in commercial proceedings

The parties in commercial disputes portrayed the state and circumstances of trade and merchant class in the first years of the Austro-Hungarian occupation. At that time, an agrarian and natural economy prevailed in Bosnia and Herzegovina, while industrial production and trade comprised only a small share of economic activity. Before the occupation, over 90% of the population was engaged in agriculture, including many residents of about fifty urban settlements. Oriental Balkan crafts and petty trade gave character to the cities of Bosnia and Herzegovina.[62] True, the reforms of the 1860s and 1870s contributed to freer economic activity and trade development, especially foreign trade (import-export trade with the Austro-Hungarian Monarchy and significant imports of oriental goods from Constantinople and other parts of the Ottoman Empire), but poor communication and transportation difficulties were major obstacles to the development of this area.[63] This level of economy and trade also experienced great setbacks due to conflicts in the period 1875–1878, as well as the war activities during the occupation in 1878.[64]

By inspecting the archival documents of the *Kreisgerichte* (county courts) and the new established Supreme Court for Bosnia and Herzegovina in Sarajevo, we can conclude that during the first years of Austro-Hungarian rule, Bosnian merchants of various denominations, Muslims, Jews and Christians, regularly appeared in commercial disputes. They often stood earlier in a business relationship (during late Ottoman times). According to the volume and manner of trade, but also wealth, merchants in Bosnia of the late Ottoman (and early Austro-Hungarian) period can be classified into three groups: small, medium and wholesalers (as the country's 'trading elite').[65] The first group includes small artisans whose business was limited to selling their own products in the bazaar *(čaršija)*. Medium-sized retailers usually had their own shop and held regional trade within Bosnia and Herzegovina – they bought goods from wholesalers once or twice a year and resold them in bazaars within the country. Large merchants (the Bosnian trading elite, consisting of family trading houses) were engaged in the import and export of goods, and usually, in addition to their main base of trading operations, also maintained shops in other cities, which operated under the auspices of commissioners and

62 *Juzbašić, Dževad*: Neke karakteristike privredno razvitka Bosne i Hercegovine u periodu od 1878. do 1914. godine, in: Juzbašić, Dževad (ed.): Politika i privreda u Bosni i Hercegovini pod austrougarskom upravom, p. 141.

63 Ibid., p. 141–142.

64 Ibid., p. 142.

65 *Younis, Hana*: op. cit., p. 57.

"guys" (momci).[66] Statistics from the post-Ottoman period confirm that the bulk of the trade class consisted of small traders who operated as sole traders, a much smaller number had two to three employees, while trading houses with more than three employees made up just over 3.6 %.[67] Although the merchant class in Bosnia and Herzegovina should be viewed as a whole – as a multi-confessional community – some differences between individual denominations existed and were conditioned by various historical, social and economic factors.[68] In addition to domestic merchants, numerous foreign entrepreneurs and trading companies (mostly from the Monarchy which entered into business relations in Bosnia after the occupation) appeared among the parties in trade disputes.

The parties were usually represented by lawyers. As a rule, these were persons from the Austro-Hungarian Monarchy who opened their law offices in Bosnia and Herzegovina. Until the enactment of the new Law of Attorneys in 1883, legal representation was not legally regulated. That is why this work was performed by various unqualified persons, which contributed to the disorderly state of court proceedings immediately after the occupation.[69] After the entry into force of the Law on Attorneys, the situation was significantly improved.

In the early post-Ottoman period (but also later), merchants came to the county courts in Bosnia and Herzegovina on various occasions. They usually registered their companies, filed for bankruptcy, filed a lawsuit, or were sued to settle a claim. Running the bankruptcy proceedings of domestic traders was one of the main tasks of the county courts. This function was taken from the earlier Ottoman commercial courts. Namely, by inspecting the Official Journal of the Bosnian Vilayet *(Bosna)* from the 1860s and 1870s, we come to the conclusion that Ottoman commercial courts regularly conducted bankruptcy proceedings of domestic merchants.[70] These courts applied bankruptcy proceedings of the Ottoman Commercial Code. This is indicated by the mentioned journal sources, in which the commercial courts cite the paragraphs of the Ottoman Commercial Code in their bankruptcy announcements.[71] As said, after 1878 bankruptcy proceedings were taken over by the newly

66 Ibid., pp. 57–58.

67 *Hauptmann, Ferdo*: Privreda i društvo Bosne i Hercegovine u doba austrougarske vladavine (1878–1918), p. 196.

68 Ibid., pp. 194–196.

69 *Eichler, Eduard*: op. cit. p. 194.

70 Conclusion based on insight into the official newspaper of the ottoman administration "Bosna" (1868–1878). Bosnian historian Hamdija Kreševljaković counted a total of 70 bankruptcies conducted by commercial courts in Bosnia from 1868 to 1878 (*Kreševjaković, Hamdija*: Stečajevi u Bosni 1867–1877, pp. 189–192).

71 In these announcements, the Commercial Court regularly referred to Articles 198, 199 and 200 and 210 of the Ottoman Commercial Code when inviting creditors to report their claims against the merchant – the bankruptcy debtor. (For example, the bankruptcy of the merchant Jova Matijević

formed county courts presided over by new judges from Austria-Hungary. This is confirmed by the official press of the new Austro-Hungarian government, in which we regularly come across court announcements about bankruptcy proceedings of merchants.[72] The newly formed courts probably also applied bankruptcy rules of the Ottoman Commercial Code (until the adoption of the new Bankruptcy Order for Bosnia and Herzegovina in 1883). As part of this research, no insight was provided into the court records of bankruptcy proceedings, but the announcements in the official press indicate that until 1883, bankruptcies were conducted according to the then formally valid Ottoman law.[73]

In addition to bankruptcy proceedings, in the court practice of the first years of the post-Ottoman period we find various disputes arising from trade transactions (made during the last decade of Ottoman rule and the first years of Austro-Hungarian rule). Common trade disputes include disputes over sales on credit (so called *veresija*). Trade on "veresija" was the basic form of trade in Bosnia in the second half of the 19th century.[74]

The sale of goods on *veresija* in the Bosnian province of the late Ottoman period was carried out in accordance with trade customs. We are informed about this by various sources. A fine description of this form of trade we find in Ahmet Dževdet-pasha's report letters from the mid 1860s. He describes how

---

announced in "Bosna" (Nr. 416 from 30 Rebiulahira 1291 – 3 (15) June 1874); bankruptcy of Banja Luka merchant Tomo Milosevic announced in "Bosna" (Nr. 495 from 21 Zilkade 1292 – 8 (20) December 1875) and many others.

72 Conclusion based on insight into the official newspaper "Sarajevski list" and "Bosansko-hercegovačke novine" (1878–1883).

73 Example of such an edict: „Vom Kreisgerichte in Sarajevo als Concursbehörde wird hiermit verlautbart: Es sei von diesem Gerichte der Concurs über das gesammte bewegliche und unbewegliche, wo immer in Bosnien und der Hercegovina befindliche Vermögen des ehemaligen Kafesieders Franz Jug in Sarajevo eröffnet, und zum Vertreter und einstweiligen Massaverwalter der hiesige Parteienvertreter Herr Georg Peleš bestellt worden. Es werden demnach alle jene Personen, die welche immer für eine Forderung an das Vermögen des in Concurs verfallenen Schuldners zu stellen haben, hiemit aufgefordert, dass dieselben ihre Forderungen längstens bis 15. April 1882 (Samstag) in Form einer Klage gegen den obgenannten Massavertreter oder die Concursmasse bei diesem Kreisgerichte anzumelden haben, widrigenfalls selbe trotz ihrer etwaigen Eigenthums,- Vorzugs- oder Pfandrechte ihrer Forderungen gegen die Concursmassa verlustig und von der Concurs-Verhandlung ausgeschlossen wären. Behufs Bestätigung des interimistischen, oder Wahl eines anderen Vermögens-Verwalters, sowie des Gläubiger-Ausschusses wird die Tagfahrt auf den 18. April 1882 (Dienstag) um 8 Uhr Früh hiergerichts, Kanzlei Nr. 2 mit dem Beifügen anberaumt, dass die Concurs-Gläubiger bei derselben um so gewisser zu erscheinen und bezüglich der Wahl des Vermögens-Verwalters und Gläubiger-Ausschusses hierbei sich zu äussern haben, widrigenfalls nach Vorschrift des Gesetzes auf die Gefahr der Gläubiger der einstweiliger Massaverwalter und Gläubiger-Ausschuss vom Gerichte aus bestellt werden würde. Kreisgericht Sarajevo, 19. Maerz 1881." (Sarajevski list, Nr. 40, 21 March (2 April) 1881).

74 *Younis, Hana*: op. cit., p. 72.

merchants from all over Bosnia come to Sarajevo, as the Vilayet's central market location. They usually go to a well-known merchant from whom they used to buy goods. If he does not have the requested goods, then that same merchant sends his buyer accompanied by his clerk to another merchant. When the buyer negotiates the price and loads the goods, the clerk issues the buyer a "note" *(cedulja)* that matches the note in the seller's trade book *(defter)*. Such trade, reports Dževdet-pasha, was carried out "without witnesses, without a stamp and without a signature",[75] i.e., without any additional certification and intervention by a state authority or a commercial court (authors note).

However, Dževdet-pasha himself notes that already at that time (mid-1860s) a new business practice was looming, which included the issuance of certified bonds and the increasing intervention of the state and the commercial courts.[76] The court records and decisions from the first years of the Austro-Hungarian administration confirm that the development of trade went in that direction. Based on the disputes before the county court in Sarajevo, it can be concluded that trade between traders was more formalized in the last decade of the Ottoman and early years of Austro-Hungarian rule. The parties who came to court usually proved their rights and claims with various documents in the form of bonds *(senet)*, trade books, bills of exchange and various certificates and documents, which were often certified or issued by courts (commercial, regular or Sharia courts).

Within this research, several disputes were found due to unpaid debt for merchandise purchased on *veresija*. Here are three examples. The first example is a lawsuit from 1883 before the Sarajevo county court – the heirs of the Muslim merchant Mustafa Janjoš sued another Muslim merchant Mula Ahmed Zelohasić and his co-debtor, the Jewish merchant Mošo Atijan, for the unpaid sum of 6,000 groschen for 36 haystacks bought "na veresiju" (on credit).[77] Another example found in the archives is a dispute between two merchants over a debt settlement – the Muslim merchant Murat Devović sued the Orthodox Nikola Glođan for the return of 2,075 groschen, which the defendant received in kind, i.e. goods (wheat, rye, hay, oats and 4 loads of raw plums).[78] The third example is the dispute initiated by the seller Emil

---

75 „Kod pregledavanja knjiga trgovačkog suda saznao sam, da provincijalni trgovci, kad dolaze podmirivati svoje potrebe, idu obično svome poznatom trgovcu, i ako u njega nema one robe, koju oni trebaju, to ih ovaj trgovac sa svojim pisarom uputi, da kod drugih trgovaca potraže robu, te kada ustanove cijenu, pokupe robu i opremaju bale. Sad pisar ispostavi kupcu cedulju, koja se podudara sa bilješkom u knjizi prodavaoca. U vrijednosti od 3 do 5 tovara groša 7) robe natovare strani trgovci na konja i nose u svoje mjesto bez ikakve druge isprave osim cedulje i knjige, koja ostaje u prodavaoca. Ovako se posluje bez svjedoka, bez žiga i bez potpisa." (*Kreševjaković, Hamdija*: Iz bosanske trgovine XIX stoljeća, p. 163).

76 *Kreševjaković, Hamdija*: Iz bosanske trgovine XIX stoljeća, p. 164.

77 ABH, VSS, Građanske parnice, 1882, 1157.

78 ABH, VSS, Građanske parnice, 1884, 10.

C. Czernowinski, owner of the company "Erstes Militär-Kleider-Magazin in Brünn – Mostar Branch", against the estate of the deceased Peter Pavičić, for uniforms and other goods purchased by the buyer in November and December 1879. The buyer was supposed to pay for the goods in installments, but he settled only part of the debt before his death.[79] The content of some of these disputes will be elaborated in more detail in the following chapters.

In addition to lawsuits due to unpaid debt for purchased goods, in the court practice, we very often encounter loan disputes between merchants. In Bosnia, for a long time during the Ottoman rule, loans were given by *waqfs* (Islamic endowments) and individuals,[80] and during the 1860s and 1870s, loans were also provided by specialized foundations, such as *menafi-sanduk* (for granting agricultural loans) and *mearif-sanduk* (school foundations).[81] Since the loans of the waqfs and the mentioned foundations were conditioned by special rules, the merchants usually practiced taking loans from wholesalers. The historical literature testifies that wholesalers in Bosnia acted as "institutional lenders".[82] This resulted in numerous disputes between merchant-lenders and merchant-borrowers who came before the regular courts during the first years of Austro-Hungarian rule. These transactions were also documented with certified bonds, so the parties proved their rights and claims in court with such documents. Examples of such disputes include the case of a dispute between plaintiff Salomon Salom, a Jewish merchant from Sarajevo, and defendant debtor Hadži[83] Mustafa Amandžija, for the payment of 1,231 forints from a loan agreement.[84] This dispute will also be presented in some detail in the next chapter, especially in the context of the application of the Ottoman rules on legal interest.

The documents used as evidence in commercial disputes were the mentioned bonds *(senet)* of the debtors, certificates of the Sharia courts (*hudžet* or *Hujjat*) and the judgments of the Sharia or regular courts of the late Ottoman or early Austro-Hungarian period. The parties sometimes proved their rights with judgments of

79 ABH, VSS, Građanske parnice, 1884, 25.

80 On the practice of granting loans by vakufs in Sarajevo from the 16th century: *Sućeska, Avdo*: Vakufski krediti u Sarajevu prema podacima iz sidžila sarajevskog kadije iz godine 973, 974. I 975/1564,65 i 66., Prilozi za orijentalnu filologiju, vol. 44–45 (1996), pp. 99–132.

81 On the menafi sanduci foundations: *Kreševjaković, Hamdija*: Menafi – sanduci (Poljodjelske pripomoćne zaklade) u Bosni i Hercegovini (1866–1878), Narodna uzdanica, vol. IX (1941), pp. 23–41 (https://www.ibn-sina.net/images/pdf/znakovi/82/61_Hamdija_Kre%C5%A1evljakovi%C4%87_znakovi82.pdf, last access: 06.06.2021).

82 *Younis, Hana*: op. cit., pp. 202–205.

83 Hadži/Hadzi (in Turkish *hacı* from Arabic *hajj* – حَجّ) – a pilgrim; for Muslims – a person who had performed the rites of the pilgrimage to Mecca; for Christians – a person who had done a pilgrimage to Jerusalem (hereinafter: H.).

84 ABH, VSS, Građanske parnice, 1884, 57.

the Ottoman Commercial Court from the 1860s and 1870s. In addition, in practice one can find lawsuits based on debts from issued invoices and excerpts from trade books, but also bills of exchange that were in circulation at the time.

From the processed archival documents we can come to the conclusion that the *senets* represented a very frequently used means of evidence of creditors in trade disputes in the late Ottoman and early post-Ottoman times. The bonds contained data on the debtor and the creditor, the amount of the debt, the payment deadline – the due date, the method of calculating interest and data on the collateral (mainly guarantors or collateral). Such bonds were certified by debtors with their seal *(muhur)* and handed over to creditors as proof of debt. Upon payment of the debt, the creditor returned this *senet* to the debtor. In addition to the certification (seal) of the debtor and the guarantor, the bonds could also be certified by state authorities (e.g. a commercial court) or by the signature (seal) of a witness.

Bonds and other documents issued in the late Ottoman period were mostly written in Arabic letters. In the first years of the Austro-Hungarian administration, such documents were submitted to the court by the parties in the original and in a translation to Bosnian (in Latin script) compiled by a certified court interpreter. This was done with the *senets*, certificates and judgments of the Sharia, regular or commercial courts, contracts, as well as all other documents that served as evidence. The following is a transcription of two *senets* from the Ottoman period, which the parties submitted to the Sarajevo county court in a commercial dispute, which was conducted during the first years of Austro-Hungarian rule.

The first example is the bond of Mula-Ahmed Zelohasić from Sarajevo, which he handed over to the seller – Sarajevo trader Mustafa-aga Janjoš – for a debt of 6,000 groschen for the purchased hay. The guarantor was Moša Žudija. The bond was issued on the 1st of Rebiulahir in 1292 (dated according to the Hijri calendar). The second bond is the *senet* of Osman-beg Zubčević, a merchant from Goražde, issued for a debt from a loan in the amount of 120 golden Ottoman lira, certified before the commercial court in 1877.

Original transcription in Bosnian of the bond of the merchant Mula-Ahmed Zelohasić issued for a debt for purchased hay on veresija in the amount of 6,000 groschen: certified by seal and witnesses in 1877.	Author's English translation of the transcription
36 plastova sijena. Samo trideset i šest plastova sijena po 300 gr.10.800 gr. U gotovini predano na račun 4.800 gr. Ostatak 6.000 gr. Samo šest hiljada groša. Povod pisanja zadužnice jest ovaj: Dugujem istinito Mustafagi Janjošu Sarajevskom žitelju od sijena osvem izdatog na račun još šest hiljada groša, te se obvezujem platiti računim (računajući) od dana datuma ovog seneta za rok od devedeset i jedan dan, slučajno ako ne bih ja na istečaj (istek) roka platio, te bi bilo potrebno sudu prijaviti, s uvjetom je, da se od moje strane naknadi sredstvom suda zajedno s glavnicom zakonita kamata za prošlo preko roka vrijeme za troškom naplate pristojbe, te usljed tog sastavim ovu jednu moju zadužnicu uručujem rečenom Mustafa agi anjošu.	36 layers of hay. Only thirty-six layers of hay per 300 gr.10,800 gr. Cash delivered 4,800 gr. The rest 6,000 gr. Only six thousand groschen. The reason for writing the debenture is: I truly owe Mustafa Janjoš, a Sarajevo resident, on the basis of hay issued on the account, another six thousand groschen, and I undertake to pay, starting from the date of this senet for a period of ninety-one days, if I do not pay accidentally on the expiration date and it would be necessary to report to the court, on the condition that through the court the main debt is settled by me together with the interest calculated for the overdue time with the expenses of fee collection added, and as a result I compile this one of my debentures to the said Mustafa aga Janjoš.
1. Rebiulahira 1292 Dužni: Mula-Ahmed Zelohasić (pečat: Ahmed) Svjedoci: Hafiz Mehmed Eff. Šerifhafizović; H. Mustafa Bakalović; H. Mehmed Mumdžija Pandžić; Mulla Jusuf Kujundžija Glasećih u zadužnici šest hiljada groša od sijena da će se s rokom od devedest i jedan dan potpuno platiti: jesam jamac i platac s tim da ako se s rokom ne nadima će se od moje strane naknaditi te ovdje označiv (označen) potvrđuje pečatom. 1. Rebiulahira 1292.Kontrakčija ambara Moše Žudija (pečat)[85]	1 Rebiulahira 1292 Obliged: Mula-Ahmed Zelohasić (stamp: Ahmed) Witnesses: Hafiz Mehmed Eff. Šerifhafizović; H. Mustafa Bakalović; H. Mehmed Mumdžija Pandžić; Mulla Yusuf Kujundzija Voting in the debenture six thousand groschen of hay that with a term of ninety-one days will be paid in full: I am a guarantor and payer with the proviso that if the term is not inflated will be reimbursed by me and marked here confirmed by a seal. 1 Rebiulahira 1292 Moshe Judia (stamp)

85 ABH, VSS, Građanske parnice, 1882, 1157. (senet dated 1 Rebiulahir 1292).

Original transcription in Bosnian of the senet of Osman-beg Zubčević issued on the basis of a loan debt in the amount of 120 gold Ottoman lira; certified before the Bosnian Commercial Court in 1877.	Author's English translation of the transcription
120 zlatnih osmanskih lira i slovom stotinu i dvadeset zlatnih osmanskih lira. Povod pisanju seneta jest ovaj: Računiv od mjeseca / 1. šubata 1292 / 13 februara 1877 godine za rok od šest mjeseci uzajmio sam, primio i prihvatio od sačuvatelja ovog seneta Judaći Efendije Isakovića sarajevskog trgovca kao što gore glasi samo stotinu i dvadeset osmanskih lira; S pomoću Božijom hoću gore rečene novce na istek rečenog roka potpuno predati i platiti, a ako to učinio ne bih te bi gore rečni povjeritelj ustao tužiti kod slavnog suda, to će se svi proizvođeni sudbeni troškovi i ostali od moje strane predati i platiti kao i kamata za vrijeme prošlo preko rečenog roka zajedno podmirit će se od moje strane, s tim uvjetom na koje se god mjesto bude džiriralo ima se primiti; te sa poznatim ostalim uvjetima jest istinit moj dug gore rečenih novaca te u svrhu toga potvrdiv ovaj moj senet predaje se gore rečenom	120 gold Ottoman lira and in letters: one hundred and twenty gold Ottoman lira. The reason for writing the senet is this: Calculated from the month / 1 šubata 1292/ 13 February 1877 for a period of six months I borrowed, received and accepted from the custodian of this senet Judaći Efendija Isaković, a Sarajevo merchant, as stated above only one hundred and twenty Ottoman lira. With God's help, I want to hand over and pay the above-mentioned money in full at the end of the said deadline, and if I do not do that, the above-mentioned creditor would sue in the glorious court. All legal costs incurred and others will be handed over and paid by me, as well as interest for the time elapsed over the said deadline with this condition to whichever place is endorsed to be received; and with known other conditions my debt of the above-mentioned money is true and for this purpose I have confirmed this my senet is given to the above mentioned
1. Šubata 1292. (13. februara 1877. godine) Osman-beg Zubčević iz Goražda (pečat: Osman) Br. 70 Izdavatelj ovog seneta Osman beg došao je u sud trgovački; te je očitovao i potvrio da se je obvezao sa označenim dugom u senetu i ostale uvete ispuniti; te dole stavljeni pečat da je njegov istinit pečat, što se i trgovačkim sudom potvrđuje (1 šubata 1292 godine) 13. februara 1877. (pečat); Bosanski trgovački sud Označenih u senetu stotinu i dvadeset osmanskih lira sa označenim uvjetima neka se na Jake Sumbulovića zapovijed plati; ja sam vrijednost potpune primio. U Sarajevu 1. Temuza 1293 (13. jula 1877.). Judaći trgovac[86]	1 Šubata 1292 (13 February 1877) Osman-beg Zubčević from Goražde (stamp: Osman) Nr. 70 The issuer of this senet, Osman Bey, came to the commercial court; and he manifested and confirmed that he had undertaken to fulfill the indicated debt in the senet and the other conditions; and the seal placed below that it is his true seal, which is also confirmed by the commercial court (1 šubata 1292) 13 February 1877 (seal); Bosnian Commercial Court One hundred and twenty Ottoman lira marked in the senate with the conditions indicated, let it be paid on Jake Sumbulović's order; I received the full value. In Sarajevo 1 Temuza 1293 (13 July 1877). Judas merchant

4. Pluralism of substantive law in commercial disputes

At the beginning of this paper, it was pointed out that the new Austro-Hungarian government in Bosnia and Herzegovina temporarily left in force the existing Ottoman law (*bestehendes heimisches Recht)* in the occupied province. This law was to

86 ABH, VSS, Građanske parnice, 1884, 4. (senet dated 13 February 1877).

be valid until it was replaced by a new law. Consequently, Ottoman commercial legislation from Tanzimat times continued its validity in Bosnia and Herzegovina until the adoption of the new Commercial Law for Bosnia and Herzegovina in 1883. In addition, other Ottoman laws and orders regulating various areas of civil law were maintained. The Ottoman Civil Code – the *Mecelle* – should have been especially important for trade and business from this group, because most of Ottoman (Sharia) law of obligations was codified in this code.[87]

Knowing that the new judges would have difficulties with the application of Ottoman law, the government supplemented the rule on the application of Ottoman law with one general exception. In special orders and instructions, in cases of legal gaps or if domestic/Ottoman law was not applicable or sufficient for decision making, judges were given the freedom to decide civil (and commercial) cases by applying analogously the laws in force in Austria-Hungary.[88] This rule paved the way for the reception of the Austrian General Civil Code (ABGB) in the jurisprudence of the regular courts in Bosnia and Herzegovina.[89] Already in the first months and years after the occupation, the new jurists and judges from the Monarchy, to whom ABGB "was in their flesh and blood", resorted to the application of this civil code.[90]

In fact, three main factors led to the sudden and very wide application of the ABGB in the practice of regular courts in the first years after the occupation. These were: 1. the fact that the ABGB was at that time the only civil law code in force in most of the Monarchy; 2. the new legal culture of new lawyers and judges sitting in the courtrooms of regular courts – the legal rules of the ABGB were easily accessible and very well known to these judges, which is why they regularly reached for them and 3. the lack of adequate translation of the Ottoman Civil Code – *Mecelle* in that period.[91]

---

87 Medželle i ahkjami šerije (Otomanski gragjanski zakon), Sarajevo 1906.

88 For example: Die Verordnung des Gemeinsamen Finanzministeriums vom 1. Januar 1879 (Band II, Justizverwaltung, p. 15): „Bis zur Erlassung neuer gesetzlicher Normen des materiellen Rechtes haben sich die Gerichtsbehörden beider Instanzen an die im Lande tatsächlich in Geltung stehende Gesetzgebung zu halten. Nur insoweit eine solche nicht besteht, oder unter den gegenwärtigen Verhältnissen unanwendbar ist, oder nicht ausreicht haben die Gerichtsbehörden ... in bürgerlichen Rechtsangelegenheiten in und ausser Streitsachen aber nach Analogie der in der österreichisch-ungarischen Monarchie in Wirksamkeit stehenden Gesetze vorzugehen".

89 *Bećić, Mehmed*: Historijska i pravna osnovanost primjene Općeg građanskog zakonika u Bosni i Hercegovini nakon okupacije 1878. godine, pp. 63–79.

90 *Pilar, Ivo*: Entwicklungsgang der Rezeption des österreichischen allgemeinen bürgerlichen Gesetzbuches in Bosnien und der Herzegovina unter besonderer Berücksichtigung des Immobilienrechtes, Festschrift zur Jahrhundertfeier des Allgemeinen bürgerlichen Gesetzbuches, 1. Juni 1911, Erster Teil, Wien 1911, p. 705.

91 For a detailed description, see e.g. *Bećić, Mehmed*: Das Privatrecht in Bosnien-Herzegowina (1878–1918), pp. 98–104; *Bećić, Mehmed*: Historijska i pravna osnovanost primjene Općeg građanskog zakonika u Bosni i Hercegovini nakon okupacije 1878. godine, pp. 63–79.; *Bećić, Mehmed*:

It can be said that the ignorance of Ottoman civil law in the first few years after the occupation led to an almost understandable application of the ABGB.[92] Only translations of certain parts of the *Mecelle* were included in the 1881 collection,[93] and it was extremely difficult for judges to get to the content of other legal rules of this code.[94] Under these circumstances, the regular courts only exceptionally applied the regulations of *Mecelle*, when it was known or available to the judge. Instead, "as a rule", the ABGB was applied, mostly in the field of contract law.[95] During the first three years, the ABGB was used as if it was formally proclaimed and in force in Bosnia and Herzegovina. The Supreme Court considered such a practice as unacceptable and incorrect. Therefore, on 28 September 1881, the Supreme Court issued a special order emphasizing that the ABGB could be applied only as a subsidiary legal source and that it was not permissible to cite paragraphs of the ABGB in the reasoning of judgments, as the code had not yet entered into force in the occupied province.[96]

Over time, the need for the application of specific institutes and rules of the *Mecelle* has arisen in legal practice. Therefore, in each specific case, the courts sent inquiries to the Provincial Government for the delivery of an official translation of certain parts and paragraphs of the Code, which were then used in specific cases.[97]

Pravni transplanti i pravni pluralizam: transformacija stvarnog prava u Bosni i Hercegovini 1878–1918, PhD thesis, Pravni fakultet Univerziteta u Sarajevu, 2018, pp. 149–161.

92 *Eichler, Eduard*: op. cit., p. 306.

93 Band II, Justizverwaltung, pp. 349–356 and Band II, Justizverwaltung, pp. 491–492.

94 Ibid., p. 186.

95 *Bećić, Mehmed*: Primjena Općeg građanskog zakonika u praksi Vrhovnog suda za Bosnu i Hercegovinu za vrijeme austrougarske uprave, master's thesis, Pravni fakultet Univerziteta u Sarajevu, 2013; *Eichler, Eduard*: op. cit., pp. 186–187 and 174; *Zobkow, Michael*: Die Anwendung des allgemeinen bürgerlichen Gesetzbuches in Bosnien und der Herzegowina, Festschrift zur Jahrhundertfeier des Allgemeinen bürgerlichen Gesetzbuches, 1. Juni 1911, Erster Teil, Wien 1911, p. 746.

96 „Unzulässig aber ist es in den Entscheidungsgründen einzelner §§ des a. b. G.B. das ist eines Gesetzes, welches in den okkupierten Provinzen noch nicht in Kraft steht zu zitieren. Da das Obergericht danach wahrgenommen hat, dass einzelne Gerichte sich nicht selten erwähnter Zitierungen bedienen, einige sich die Arbeit sogar in der Weise bequemer machen, dass sie sich darauf beschränken nur den bezüglichen § nicht aber auch die gesetzliche Bestimmung, die er enthält ihrem Inhalte nach anzuführen, ergeht an alle Gerichte die strengste Weisung, in hierkunft mehrerwähnte Zitierungen, dort wo sie nicht am Platze sind/: Instruktion über die Behandlung, der v. den k.u.k.österr.ung. Konsulaten übernommenen Agenden vom 26. Mai 1880 No = 9276/2065 J:/ zu vermeiden. Ist es doch höchst sonderbar, dasjenige, was Rechtens ist, durch ein Recht zu begründen, welches in Bezug auf die betreffende Partei gar nicht zu Recht besteht, und ihr gar noch zuzumuthen, sich, da ihr die Bestimmung des fraglichen §. doch nicht bekannt sein kann, bei dem Wortlaute des Gesetzes Rat einzuholen ..." (Sammlung der Justiznormalien für Bosnien und die Hercegovina, Band I, Jahrgang 1878–1885, Nr. 171).

97 *Bećić, Mehmed*: Primjena Medželle u postosmanskoj Bosni i Hercegovini, pp. 57–58.

After 1890, the translation of the entire code was completed,[98] but its use in practice was problematic.[99] In an order from 1893, the Provincial Government emphasized that these translations served only as information on the contents of the *Mecelle*,[100] while in a decision from 1892 the Supreme Court pointed out that the translations of the *Mecelle* were not reliable enough "that the decision of a particular case could be based on them".[101] This did not lead to major changes. It remained for the court to assess whether the rules of the *Mecelle* and domestic law in general were applicable and to decide how much of that law will be taken into account when deciding in each particular case.[102] Excluded from this were those issues for which the ABGB had meanwhile came into force (e.g. reception through the land registry institute and some others).[103]

This concept of application of substantive civil law led to coexistence – the simultaneous application of Ottoman civil law and the Austrian ABGB, which contributed to a great deal of legal uncertainty in legal practice. It was particularly difficult to determine the extent and limits of the coexistence of the *Mecelle* and the ABGB.[104] We learn from many sources that this legal uncertainty was a serious problem for courts, parties and lawyers in Bosnia and Herzegovina.[105] A certain degree of unification of court practice was achieved gradually through the decisions and practice of the Supreme Court.[106] Many of its decisions insisted on the application of domestic law, while the application of the ABGB was supposed to be supplementary/subsidiary. Thus, the longest continuity of application of *Mecelle* was maintained in those specific rules and institutes that were not known or otherwise regulated by Austrian law. For example, rules on legal capacity, legal acts during the terminal illness *(maraz-mevt)*, the rule that purchase does not break rent, statute

98 *Sladović, Eugen*: Islamsko pravo u Bosni i Hercegovini, Beograd 1926, p. 28.

99 *Bećić, Mehmed*: Primjena Medželle u postosmanskoj Bosni i Hercegovini, p. 59.

100 Circularerlass der Landesregierung Nr. 71.835/III vom 9. August 1893. an das Obergericht, die Kreisgerichte und Bezirksbehörden, Sammlung der Justiznormalien für Bosnien und die Hercegovina, Band III, Jahrgang 1891–1895, pp. 1454–1455.

101 Decision of the Supreme Court for BH dated 24 March 1892 (Präjudicienbuch in Civilsachen, Band II, Sammlung der Entscheidungen aus den Jahren: 1890, 1891, 1892, 1893, 1894 und 1895, Obergericht für Bosnien und die Hercegovina, Sarajevo 1899, Nr. 225).

102 *Ajsner, Bertold*: O općem građanskom pravu u Bosni i Hercegovini, Preštampano iz „Arhiva" za pravne i društvene nauke, Beograd 1920, p. 11; *Shek, Adalbert*: Uvod u predavanja o bosanskohercegovačkom pravu, Mjesečnik Pravničkog društva u Zagrebu, vol. I (1914), no. 2, p. 100.

103 *Bećić, Mehmed*: Historijska i pravna osnovanost primjene Općeg građanskog zakonika u Bosni i Hercegovini nakon okupacije 1878. godine, pp. 63–79.

104 See: *Bećić, Mehmed*: Das Privatrecht in Bosnien-Herzegowina (1878–1918), p. 103.

105 For example *Zobkow, Michael*: op. cit., p. 732; *Bećić, Mehmed*: Historijska i pravna osnovanost primjene Općeg građanskog zakonika u Bosni i Hercegovini nakon okupacije 1878. godine, pp. 63–79.

106 *Eichler, Eduard*: op. cit., pp. 307–308.

of limitations etc.[107] The complete rejection of *Mecelle* came only gradually in the post-annexation period, that is, in the second decade of the 20th century, when the Provincial Government gave wider powers to judges to apply the ABGB.[108]

The described pluralism of legal sources was also reflected in trade disputes in the early post-Ottoman period. Namely, even before the entry into force of the Commercial Law for Bosnia and Herzegovina in 1883 (ADHGB reception),[109] the courts regularly resorted to the application of the ABGB in resolving commercial disputes. In addition to the ABGB, which served as an additional source for judges to deal with certain issues (mainly the law of obligations), the courts applied Ottoman (domestic) law to some other issues. Thus, for example, statutes of limitations were regularly calculated according to Ottoman law and compensation for damages (legal interest) was recognized according to the provisions of the Appendix to the Ottoman Commercial Code of 1860. In the following text, two cases from the court practice of the early post-Ottoman period will be reconstructed. These cases show how the ABGB was applied in commercial disputes.

The first example is a dispute from 1883. Muslim merchant Murat Devović sued the Christian merchant Nikola Glođan for the return of 2,075 groschen for unjust enrichment, which the plaintiff handed over to the defendant in goods (wheat, rye, hay, oats and raw plums). The plaintiff decided to file this lawsuit only after he was convicted (Judgment of 8 July 1883) to pay the defendant the amount of 2,082 groschen due to the debt documented in a *senet* of 14 May 1868. The plaintiff claimed that it was for the purpose of settling that debt from 1868 that he handed over the above-mentioned goods to the defendant. However, since he is now sentenced to pay that same debt, he filed a lawsuit against the defendant for unjust enrichment for the received goods with the value of 2,075 groschen. On the other hand, the defendant claimed that he included the received goods in the plaintiff's earlier debt. Thus, the defendant claimed that the plaintiff had another debt of 2,082 groschen, for which he was later legally sentenced to payment.[110]

The first-instance court ordered the defendant Nikola Glođaj to pay the plaintiff a "mutual natural purchase" in the amount of 166 forints, i.e. 2,075 groschen. The

107 For example: *Zobkow, Michael*: op. cit., pp. 747–751.

108 For example: *Bećić, Mehmed*: Pravni transplanti i pravni pluralizam: transformacija stvarnog prava u Bosni i Hercegovini 1878–1918, p. 156; *Ajsner, Bertold*: op. cit., pp. 21–22, 24; Verordnung der Landesregierung vom 27. Oktober 1911. (ABH, ZVS, Prez, 5527, 1911. (4474/praes, 1911.)).

109 After the entry into force of the Commercial Law for BH in 1883, the Austrian General Civil Code was regularly used as a supplementary source, in accordance with Article 1 of the Commercial Law (See: *Schön, Josef*: Das bosnisch-herzegowinische, österreichische, ungarische und kroatische Handelsrecht in ihren Verschiedenheiten: ein vergleichender und ergänzender Kommentar zum Handelsgesetze für Bosnien und die Herzegowina, Wien 1913, pp. 3–4).

110 ABH, VSS, Građanske parnice, 1884, 10. (Nr. 1: judgment of the Court in Foča dated 20 October 1883).

court based its decision on the fact that the defendant could not show the trade books from which it would be clear that the debt arose before the mentioned document from 1868. In addition, the court based its decision on testimonies of the plaintiff's witnesses.[111] However, the appellate court decided to temporarily dismiss the plaintiff with his claim. The court found that the plaintiff had not yet paid the amount he was ordered to pay, so the conditions for filing a lawsuit had not yet been met. It is clear from the reasoning of the judgment that the court adhered to Austrian civil law, assessing that the plaintiff did not meet all the conditions for filing a lawsuit for "paying a non-debt" *(plaćanje neduga)*, calling the lawsuit *indebiti solutio*.[112]

This case shows the approach of a regular court in civil and commercial cases: the legal gap is filled by the application of ABGB rules, although the court decision does not cite the ABGB paragraphs. On the other hand, the earlier process indicates that the statute of limitations was respected in accordance with Ottoman law (15 years), which is clearly indicated by the decision passed on the basis of the *senet* from 1868.

Another example that shows the application of ABGB rules in commercial cases is the dispute between two Sarajevo entrepreneurs: Josef Poliok, an entrepreneur, and the defendant Jakob Kampus "Čolo", who is mentioned in the documents as an entrepreneur – butcher. On 20 May 1883, they entered into a contract according to which the defendant was obliged, "to sell good and healthy meat without any complaints" for a price that "would always be a quarter cheaper than the official limit price". The plaintiff was obliged to obtain his beef exclusively from the defendant. As a deposit for the correct observance of the contract, the plaintiff gave the defendant two lots (one *Theissloos* and one *Serbenloos*). The duration of the contract was established on 3 December 1883.[113]

In the lawsuit of 18 July 1883, the plaintiff asserted that the defendant repeatedly delivered meat that did not comply with the contract and that the delivery was not on time, and from 13 July 1883 did not deliver at all. Therefore, the plaintiff demanded the termination of the contract and the restitution of the lots handed over as caution.[114] In the course of the proceedings, the defendant recognized the contract, but claimed "to have complied with the provisions of the contract for the delivery of meat".[115]

In its judgment of 24 August 1883, the county court in Sarajevo dismissed the complaint on the following grounds:

---

111 Ibid.

112 ABH, VSS, Građanske parnice, 1884, 10. (judgment of the Court in Sarajevo dated 15 January 1884).

113 ABH, VSS, Građanske parnice, 1884, 35. (contract dated 20 May 1883).

114 ABH, VSS, Građanske parnice, 1884, 35. (lawsuit dated 18 July 1883).

115 ABH, VSS, Građanske parnice, 1884, 35. (reasoning of the judgment dated 18 July 1883).

"If one party does not perform the contract at all or not at the appropriate time in the appropriate place or in the stipulated manner; except in the cases specified in the law or an expressed reservation, according to the law, the other party is not entitled to demand the cancellation, but only the exact fulfillment of the contract and compensation.
The present case does not belong to those in which the law permits the cancellation of the contract ... nor is it contained in the contract that the parties have reserved the right to cancel the contract in the event of improper performance … the Plaintiff's request therefore has to be dismissed; however, he is free to take legal action against the other party for exact fulfillment of the contract and compensation."[116]

Thus, here too, the court complied with the ABGB rules on the consequences of non-performance of the contract. Although there is no mention of the ABGB in the judgment and reasoning, it is clear that the court in its reasoning almost literally copied the legal rule of Article 918 of the ABGB. The plaintiff appealed the decision to the Supreme Court in Sarajevo. In his appeal of 12 September 1883, filed through attorney Moritz Weiss, the plaintiff also relied on the ABGB rules.[117] But, the Supreme Court dismissed the appeal.[118]

5. Continuity of rules on compensation of damages from the Ottoman Commercial Code

The Ottoman Commercial Code of 9 Sheval 1276 (1860) was supplemented by an Appendix which contained additional legal rules, mainly on the organization and operation of commercial courts.[119] In addition, the Appendix contained two

---

116 „Nach dem Gesetze ist der eine Teil, wenn der andere Teil den Vertrag gar nicht oder nicht nur zur gehörigen Zeit an dem gehörigen Orte oder auf die bedungene Weise erfüllt; ausser den im dem Gesetze bestimmten Fällen oder einem ausdrücklichen Vorbehalte nicht berechtigt die Aufhebung, sondern nur die genaue Erfüllung des Vertrages und den Ersatz zu fordern. Der vorliegende Fall gehört aber nicht zu den jenigen in welchen das Gesetz die Aufhebung des Vertrages gestattet, ... noch ist dieß im Vertrage enthalten, daß sich die Partheien die Auflösung des Vertrages im Falle der nicht gehörigen Erfüllung vorbehalten haben und es mußte deshalb der Kläger mit seinem Begehren abgewiesen werden; es steht ihm jedoch frei gegen den Belangten auf genaue Erfüllung des Vertrages und Ersatz klagbar aufzutreten." (ABH, VSS, Građanske parnice, 1884, 35. (reasoning of the judgment dated 18 July 1883)).

117 ABH, VSS, Građanske parnice, 1884, 35. (appeal dated 12 September 1883).

118 ABH, VSS, Građanske parnice, 1884, 35. (decision of the Supreme Court dated 20 October 1883).

119 I. Einleitende Bestimmungen, II. Von der Organisation der Handelsgerichte, III. Von der Competenz der Handelsgerichte, IV. Von der inneren Geschäftsordnung der Handelsgerichte, V. Von der Organisation des Appelhofes in Constantinopel (Band II, Justizverwaltung, pp. 439–450).

more sections, in which we find rules of substantive law: section VI Bill of exchange protests and section VII Compensation of damages.[120] The Appendix to the Ottoman Commercial Code was published in German translation by the new Austro-Hungarian government in Bosnia and Herzegovina, together with other Ottoman laws in the aforementioned 1881 Collection of Laws and Orders for Bosnia and Herzegovina.[121]

Therefore, in addition to the procedural rules, the Appendix also contained certain substantive legal rules, which included rules on compensation of damages. Although these articles are entitled as "compensation of damages" (in German translation *Vom Schadensersatz*), a careful reading of the legal provisions leads to the conclusion that these articles regulate, in fact, statutory interest. This conclusion follows from Article 99 of the Appendix:

> "In the case of contracts limited to the payment of a certain sum, the compensation for delay in fulfillment consists only in the condemnation of legal interests of 12 percent annually. This compensation is due without the creditor having to prove a loss. It is due only from the day of protest, if one was raised, or from the day of the complaint, if it was not stipulated in the act itself or if it is legally valid."[122]

The rules on damages and statutory interest of the Ottoman Commercial Code (Appendix) were obviously deeply rooted in the consciousness of the local population, but also in business and legal practice in Bosnia during the second half of the 19th century. It could be said that these rules of the Ottoman commercial law represented the living law of domestic legal and business transactions in the second half of the 19th century. This was the case for the late Ottoman and post-Ottoman (Austro-Hungarian) era. It should be emphasized here that Bosnia and Herzegovina were no exception. Other countries had a similar business practice in the late Ottoman period, as some historical studies indicate.[123]

---

120 Band II, Justizverwaltung, pp. 450–452 (Von den Wechselprotesten; Vom Schadensersatz).

121 Even before that (22 July 1880), the sixth section (Von den Wechselprotesten) was republiced by the Provincial Government in a special decree with a minor amendment to Article 87 (Band II, Justizverwaltung, p. 450).

122 „Bei Verträgen, die sich auf die Zahlung einer bestimmten Summe beschränken, besteht der Schadenersatz aus Verzögerung der Erfüllung lediglich in der Verurtheilung zu den gesetzlichen Interessen von 12 Percent jährlich. Dieser Schadenersatz gebührt, ohne dass der Gläubiger einen Verlust nachweisen müsste. Er gebührt nur vom Tage des Protestes, wenn ein solcher erhoben wurde, oder vom Tage der Decretirung der Klage, falls er nicht im Acte selbst stipulirt gewesen oder nach dem Gesetze von Rechtswegen läuft." (Band II, Justizverwaltung, p. 452).

123 *Ade, Mafalda*: Ottoman Commercial Law and Its Application in Aleppo Province (1850–1880), in: Faroqhi, Suraiya/Veinstein, Gilles (eds.): Merchants in the Ottoman Empire, Leuven 2008, pp. 243–258.

Archival sources in the form of bonds, lawsuits and court decisions confirm the fact that the provisions of the seventh section of the Appendix to the Ottoman Commercial Code were part of the living law of Bosnia. Namely, during the first years of the Austro-Hungarian administration, we encounter numerous court disputes in which the plaintiffs-creditors regularly demanded *legal interest* (as they are called in the lawsuit) in accordance with Ottoman law. The parties regularly demanded 12% annual interest either from the date of filing the lawsuit or from the date of maturity of the debt (when the lawsuit was based on a document stipulating the obligation to pay interest from the date of maturity – usually bonds).

Looking into archival sources and court decisions makes it clear that regular courts, headed by new judges from the Monarchy, applied the rules of the seventh section of the Appendix when resolving various disputes (not just those from commercial relations). The following is a reconstruction of several such trials.

The first example is the before mentioned case of Mula Ahmed Zelohasić over a debt for 36 haystacks sold on *veresija* for 6,000 groschen. Plaintiffs – heirs of the deceased Muslim merchant Mustafa Janjoš – sued the buyer Mula Ahmed Zelohasić as the main debtor and the Jew Moša Atijan (as guarantor) for the payment of the debt and interest in the amount of 12% from the due date of debt. The plaintiff's claim dates back to Ottoman times and was proved by a bond – senet (from 1 Rebiul ahir 1292) in which the obligation to pay legal interest "for the time overdue" ("za prošlo preko roka vrijeme") is indicated.[124] Even before the occupation, the seller sued the said guarantor before the commercial court. In 1877 the commercial court in Sarajevo sentenced the guarantor to pay this debt.[125] However, as it turned out that he was over-indebted and had no property, the plaintiffs dropped the lawsuit against this guarantor and sued only the main debtor.[126] The court in Sarajevo accepted the plaintiff's claim and on 25 May 1883, sentenced the main debtor, i.e. the buyer Mula Ahmed Zelohasic, to pay 6,000 groschen and 12% interest from the due date of the main debt.[127] After the defendant filed an appeal, the decision was confirmed by the Supreme Court for Bosnia and Herzegovina on 12 August 1883.[128]

Another example is the dispute between two traders from Sarajevo, plaintiff Hilmi-aga Kapetanović and defendant Mula Husein Bećarević. The plaintiff claimed 70 Ottoman gold lira and 400 groschen for merchandise sold on credit ("na vere-

---

124 ABH, VSS, Građanske parnice, 1882, 1157. (senet dated 1 Rebiul ahir 1292).

125 ABH, VSS, Građanske parnice, 1882, 1157. (decision of the Commercial Court in Sarajevo dated 3 April 1877).

126 ABH, VSS, Građanske parnice, 1882, 1157. (court record dated 20 March 1883).

127 ABH, VSS, Građanske parnice, 1882, 1157. (judgment dated 12 August 1883).

128 ABH, VSS, Građanske parnice, 1882, 1157. (judgment dated 12 August 1883).

siju") and 12% interest from the day of the lawsuit until payment.[129] It was a claim from 1872, and the main plaintiffs evidence was a "hujjet" – certificate of the Sharia court dated 25 July 1872. As collateral, the debtor pledged his real estate.[130] In its decision from 8 October 1884, the court sentenced the defendant to pay the debt and interest in the amount of 12% from the day the lawsuit was filed.[131] It is clear, therefore, that in this dispute the court complied with the rules of the Ottoman commercial law on statutory interest. In addition, the said court decision indicates that the court applied the statute of limitations rules in accordance with Ottoman civil law *(Mecelle)*.

The rules of Section VII of the Appendix to the Commercial code (rules on compensation/legal interest) were applied in practice to various legal relations and transactions. In the court practice we find a number of disputes arising from loan agreements between merchants. In any case, here, too, interest was regularly sought and decided in accordance with Ottoman law. The following are two examples from the early post-Ottoman period:

The plaintiff sought payment of a debt on the basis of a loan agreement concluded in the post-Ottoman period (debenture dated 5 May 1883). In addition to the payment of the debt, the plaintiff also demanded interest from the due date of the obligation (6 September 1883) until payment of the debt. However, in the judgment of 24 March 1884, the court in Sarajevo sentenced the defendant to pay 270 forints with 12% interest, but from the day of the lawsuit until the payment. In the reasoning of the decision, the court emphasized that the interest "in terms of the time since it flowed, could be awarded only from the day of the lawsuit under the regulation of Section VII of the Commercial Law of 9 Sheval 1276, because interest was not agreed and the claim was not protested."[132]

Another case is a loan concluded between two wholesalers in the late Ottoman period. Salomon Salom, a Sarajevo merchant sued H. Mustafa Amandžija for payment of 1,231 forints, with 12% interest from the due date of the obligation.[133] The plaintiff based his claim on a bond (senet) issued in 1874, in which Hadži Mustafa Amandžija, as a guarantor and payer (for the main debtor M. Abdija Music), undertook to pay 218 ducats. Interest was contracted only in the case of late payment of the main debt – in which case the interest was to be calculated from the due date of the obligation until payment (as stated in the claim).[134] The Sarajevo court, presided by Judge Lavoslav Vragovic, ruled in favor of the plaintiff. In its decision

129 ABH, VSS, Građanske parnice, 1884, 186. (lawsuit of Hilmi-aga Kapetanović).

130 ABH, VSS, Građanske parnice, 1884, 186. (hudžet dated 7 August 1871).

131 ABH, VSS, Građanske parnice, 1884, 186. (judgment dated 27 August 1884).

132 ABH, VSS, Građanske parnice, 1884, 89.

133 ABH, VSS, Građanske parnice, 1884, 57.

134 ABH, VSS, Građanske parnice, 1884, 57. (Schuldschein – senet dated 30 November 1874).

from 4 February 1884, the court decided that the defendant was obliged to pay 1,231 forints with 12% interest from 30 November 1875.[135]

The Ottoman interest rate of 12% for trade was abolished with the new Commercial Law for Bosnia and Herzegovina. This means that from 1 November 1883 the 12% legal interest rate of Ottoman law ceased to be valid for trade transactions (in the sense of Article 284 of the new Commercial Law for Bosnia and Herzegovina). Namely, Article 301 of the Commercial Law halved the interest rate and set it at 6%, while higher interest rates could be agreed between the parties. The complete legal regulation of the area of interest was resolved with special laws in 1907 (revised in 1912).[136]

Disputes over the amount of legal interest were recorded after the entry into force of the new Commercial Law in 1883. We can see this by looking at cases of the courts and the Supreme Court for Bosnia and Herzegovina.

For example, the trading company of Leopold Engelman ("Exp. Engelman & Co.") from Budapest sued the Sarajevo trader Salomon Elias Kabiglio for the rest of the purchase price for goods purchased on credit ("na veresiju") in the amount of over 579 forints and paying legal interest in the amount of 12 %. The plaintiff proved his claim with an excerpt from the "properly and regularly kept trade books". The lawsuit was filed on 27 July 1884, on behalf of the plaintiff by Sarajevo lawyer Berthold Krasa. The court decided that the Sarajevo trader had to pay the rest of the purchase price for the purchased goods. However, the court reduced the amount of interest claimed to 6% within the meaning of Article 301 of the new Commercial Code for Bosnia and Herzegovina, with the explanation that the claim arose from a transaction which was considered a commercial transaction, in accordance with Article 284 of the Commercial Law.

The decisions of the Supreme Court for Bosnia and Herzegovina also show that there were disputes about the interest rate and application of Ottoman commercial law rules. For example, in the decision of 8 November 1888 it is stated:

> "According to Art. 99 Turkish Commercial law from 9 Scheval 1276 – 12% interest has to be calculated; after 1 November 1883, the day on which the Commercial law for Bosnia and Herzegovina came into force – only 6% interest is allowed to be charged, higher interest rates have to be reduced to the legal level according to the law of 16 Scheval 1280. Charging interest from interest is not permitted."[137]

---

135 ABH, VSS, Građanske parnice, 1884, 57. (judgment dated 4 February1884).

136 Gesetz- und Verordnungsblatt für Bosnien und die Hercegovina, Jahrgang 1907, Sarajevo 1908, pp. 237–239 and 239–240.

137 Decision of the Supreme Court for BH dated 8 November 1888: „Zu Handelsgeschäften sind nach Art. 99 türkischen H.G. vom 9. Scheval 1276 – 12% Zinsen zu rechnen; vom 1. November 1883, dem Tage an dem das Handelsgesetz für Bosnien und Herzegovina in Kraft getreten ist – nur 6%

In the court practice of the Supreme Court we find many decisions that refer to the rules of Section VII of the Appendix to the Ottoman Commercial Code. For example, in the judgment from 29 April 1887, the Supreme Court based his decision on Articles 91, 92 and 99 of the Ottoman Commercial Code (Appendix), when it stated:

> "If the judgment has been made on payment of the capital, a claim for interest can be made with a special legal action; in the absence of a reminder, the interest is to be awarded from the day the legal action (for payment of the debt) is handled (Art. 91, 92, 99 Law from 9 Sheval 1276)."[138]

It can be concluded that these Ottoman commercial law rules had general validity and were applied to various legal relations and affairs. The Supreme Court for Bosnia and Herzegovina took such a position in a decision dated 5 November 1885. Thus, for example, the application of Ottoman commercial law rules on interest/compensation can be found in decisions on compensation for damage caused by nullity of a sales of property contract,[139] damage caused by the theft of an object,[140] damages caused by other criminal offenses etc.[141]

Interessen zu berechnen zulässig, höher aufgerechnete Zinsen sind nach Gesetz vom 16. Scheval 1280 auf das gesetzliche Mass zu reduciren. Zinsen von Zinsen zu berechnen ist unstatthaft." (Präjudicienbuch in Civilsachen, Band I, Obergericht für Bosnien und die Hercegovina, Sarajevo 1899, Nr. 1242).

138 Decision of the Supreme Court for BH dated 29 April 1887: „Ist das Urtheil auf Zahlung des Capitals ergangen, so kann mit besonderer Klage der Anspruch auf Zinsen gestellt werden, die Zinsen sind mangels Mahnung – vom Tage der Behändigung der Klage auf Zahlung der Schuld zuzusprechen (91, 92, 99 Ges. 9. Scheval 1276)." (Präjudicienbuch in Civilsachen, Band I, Obergericht für Bosnien und die Hercegovina, Nr. 910).

139 Decision of the Supreme Court for BH dated 4 April 1888: „Ein gegen die Vorschrift des § 36 d. Ramazangesetzes geschlossener Veräusserungsvertrag ist nichtig – aus einem solchen Vertrage hat jede Partei das Erhaltene zurückzustellen, und zwar der Verkäufer den Kaufschilling mit 12% Zinsen vom tage der Zustellung der Klage an im Sinne des § 91, 99 des Gesetzes vom 9. Scheval 1276. Das Urteil hat den Klagegrund zu enthalten" (Präjudicienbuch in Civilsachen, Band I, Obergericht für Bosnien und die Hercegovina, Nr. 1187).

140 Decision of the Supreme Court for BH dated 25 February 1885: „Interesssen sind zu einem zugesprochenen Schadensersatzbetrag für gestohlenes Gut in Gemässheit des § 95 ottom. H. G. als entgangener Gewinn von der gestohlenen Summe zuzusprechen" (Präjudicienbuch in Civilsachen, Band I, Obergericht für Bosnien und die Hercegovina, Nr. 198).

141 Decision of the Supreme Court for BH dated 25 February 1885: „Die mit der Verfolgung des Diebstahls verbundenen nothwendigen Auslagen sind als Schadenersatz zuzusprechen." (Präjudicienbuch in Civilsachen, Band I, Obergericht für Bosnien und die Hercegovina, Nr. 201).

Often such decisions indicate legal pluralism, i.e. pluralism of legal sources on which the court made its decisions.[142] For example, in one of his decisions, the Supreme Court cited the rules of ABGB, *Mecelle* and Ottoman commercial law, giving preference to domestic (Ottoman law) in the application of the rules on statute of limitation and interest:

> "1) In Ottoman law, there is no prohibition ne ultra alterum tantum (§ 1335 ABGB) with regard to interest. 2) According to domestic law, past interest claims do not expire in three years (§ 1480 ABGB) but in fifteen years (§ 1660 Mecelle). 3) The reminder of the interest payment is not required if the interest obligation is based on a contract (Article 92 Appendix of the Law from 9 Sheval 1276 Collection Volume II page 452)."[143]

6. Concluding remarks

During the second half of the 19th century, Bosnia and Herzegovina went through two phases of commercial law reform. The first was the judicial and legal reform under Ottoman rule, during the Tanzimat era. The second reform is related to the transplantation/reception of Austrian and Hungarian commercial law, i.e. the process of unification of commercial law under Austro-Hungarian rule. In this paper, I sought to reconstruct commercial disputes and investigate the application of Ottoman commercial law in Bosnia and Herzegovina in the early post-Ottoman period. In the following, I will summarize the results of the research presented in this paper.

---

142 Decision of the Supreme Court for BH dated 6 March 1888: „Umfang des Schadensersatzes aus strafbarer Handlung. Der verurtheilte Geklagte hat den Anspruch auf Rückforderung ‚alles geleisteten' falls der Eid, welchen der Kläger abgelegt hatte als falsch erklärt worden ist (§ 1435 a.b.G.B.). Als Ersatz gebührt nebst dem geleisteten Betrage der nachgewiesene Schaden und Gewinnsentgang, welcher nicht einfach in den gesetzlichen Zinsen besteht, und sind die gesetzlichen Zinsen als Ersatz und Gewinnsentgang nur dann zuzusprechen, wenn ein höherer Anspruch nicht nachgewiesen wird. Die gesetzlichen Zinsen betragen in diesem Falle 12% nach 91, 99 Gesetz vom 9. Schewal 1275." (Präjudicienbuch in Civilsachen, Band I, Obergericht für Bosnien und die Hercegovina, Nr. 1047).

143 Decision of the Supreme Court for BH dated 8 August 1892: „1) Nach ottomanischem Recht besteht bezüglich der Zinsen kein Verboth ne ultra alterum tantum (§ 1335 a.b.G.B.). 2) Nach einheimischem Recht verjähren die Vorderungen der rückständigen Zinsen nicht in drei Jahren (§ 1480 a.b.G.B.) sondern in fünfzen Jahren (§ 1660 Medzelle). 3) Es ist die Mahnung der Zinsenzahlung nicht erforderlich, wenn die Zinspflicht auf einem Vertrag beruht (Art. 92 Anhang zum Gesetz vom 9. Scheval 1276 Slg. Bd. II Seite 452.)" (Präjudicienbuch in Civilsachen, Band II, Obergericht für Bosnien und die Hercegovina, Nr. 270).

1. During the Tanzimat period, special commercial courts were introduced throughout the Ottoman Empire. The function of these courts was to deal with commercial cases in accordance with the new Ottoman commercial legislation (based on French law). Despite the difficult implementation of the Tanzimat, the Ottoman government managed to establish such commercial courts in Vilayet Bosna. Thus, the organization of the Ottoman commercial courts in Bosnia did not remain a dead letter. The law in action perspective indicates that the Ottoman commercial courts in Bosnia functioned and applied the new Ottoman commercial law.

After the Austro-Hungarian occupation of Bosnia and Herzegovina, the Ottoman commercial courts were abolished. Already in the first orders on the organization of courts the new government ordered that special commercial courts were to be abolished and that commercial cases were to be transferred to the jurisdiction of regular courts. The staffing of the regular courts was significantly different compared with the Ottoman era. Instead of Ottoman judges and domestic merchants, commercial cases were now decided by judges from Austria-Hungary. Unlike the lowest, district courts, older and more experienced lawyers were appointed to the positions of higher courts, i.e. county courts *(Kreisgerichte)* and the newly formed Supreme Court for Bosnia and Herzegovina *(Obergericht für Bosnien und die Herzegovina)*. In addition, in these higher courts, decisions were made by judicial councils (senates). All this ensured a greater degree of legal certainty, legal knowledge and legal skills in resolving commercial cases.

The new Austro-Hungarian government decided to temporarily maintain the existing Ottoman law in Bosnia and Herzegovina. The old Ottoman law was to be valid until new laws were imposed for Bosnia and Herzegovina. In order for this principle to be implemented in practice, the new administration prepared and published German translations of Ottoman commercial laws from the Tanzimat era. In this way, the Austro-Hungarian authorities provided the basic legal and technical conditions for the continued validity and application of Ottoman commercial legislation in Bosnia and Herzegovina. These commercial laws remained in force until they were replaced in 1883 by new laws – legal transplants of Austrian/Hungarian/German commercial legislation. Thus, Ottoman commercial law ceased to be valid at the end of 1883. The exceptions were obviously the statutory provisions for damages (i.e. statutory interest) from the Appendix to the Ottoman Commercial Code of 1860.

2. A brief look at the courtroom of regular courts showed us that the parties in commercial disputes portrayed the state and circumstances of trade and merchant class in the first years of the Austro-Hungarian occupation. By inspecting the archival documents of the *Kreisgerichte* (county courts) and the new established Supreme Court for Bosnia and Herzegovina in Sarajevo, we can conclude that during the first years of Austro-Hungarian rule, Bosnian merchants of various

denominations, Muslims, Jews and Christians, regularly appeared in commercial disputes. In addition to domestic merchants, numerous foreign entrepreneurs and trading companies (mostly from the Monarchy) appeared among the parties in commercial disputes.

In the early post-Ottoman period (but also later), merchants came to the county courts on various occasions. They usually registered their companies, filed for bankruptcy, filed a lawsuit, or were sued to settle a claim. Most common trade disputes include disputes over sales on credit (so called *veresija*), which was the basic form of trade in Bosnia in the second half of the 19th century.

The documents used as evidence in commercial disputes were bonds *(senet)* of the debtors, certificates of the Sharia courts *(hudžet)* and the judgments of the Sharia or regular courts of the late Ottoman or early Austro-Hungarian period. The parties sometimes proved their rights with judgments of the Ottoman Commercial Court from the 1860s and 1870s, issued invoices, excerpts from trade books *(defter)*, but also bills of exchange that were in circulation at the time.

3. When it comes to the substantive law, on the basis of which the courts made their decisions in commercial disputes, the phenomenon of legal pluralism was pointed out. The new Austro-Hungarian government temporarily left in force the existing Ottoman law in Bosnia and Herzegovina. Consequently, Ottoman commercial legislation from the Tanzimat era continued its validity until the adoption of the new Commercial Law for Bosnia and Herzegovina in 1883. In addition, other Ottoman laws and orders regulating various areas of civil law were maintained, like the Ottoman Civil Code – *Mecelle*, which contained most of Ottoman (Sharia) law of obligations. But, knowing that the new judges would have difficulties with the application of Ottoman law, the government supplemented the rule on the application of Ottoman law with one general exception: If domestic/Ottoman law was not applicable or sufficient for decision making, judges were given the freedom to decide civil (and commercial) cases by applying analogously the laws in force in Austria-Hungary. This rule paved the way for the reception of the Austrian General Civil Code (ABGB) in the court practice of regular courts in Bosnia and Herzegovina.

This concept of application of substantive civil law led to coexistence – the simultaneous application of Ottoman civil law and the Austrian ABGB. Namely, the courts regularly resorted to the application of the ABGB in resolving commercial disputes. In addition to the ABGB, which served as an additional source for judges to deal with certain issues (mainly in the law of obligations), the courts applied Ottoman (domestic) law to some other issues. Thus, for example, statutes of limitations were regularly calculated according to Ottoman law *(Mecelle)* and compensation for damages (statutory interest) was recognized according to the provisions of the Appendix to the Ottoman Commercial Code of 1860.

4. The rules on damages/statutory interest of the Appendix to the Ottoman Commercial Code were obviously deeply rooted in the consciousness of the local population, but also in commercial and legal practice in Bosnia during the second half of the 19th century. During the first years of the Austro-Hungarian administration, we find numerous court disputes in which the plaintiff-creditors regularly demanded statutory interest (as described in the lawsuit) in accordance with Ottoman law. Archival sources and court decisions make it clear that regular courts, headed by new judges from the Monarchy, applied the rules of Section VII of the Appendix when resolving various disputes (not just those from commercial relations). It could be said that these rules of the Ottoman commercial law represented the living law of domestic legal and business transactions in the second half of the 19th century. This was the case for the late Ottoman and post-Ottoman (Austro-Hungarian) era.

Ivelina Masheva

Legal and Judicial Reforms in an Imperial and Post-Imperial Setting: Commercial Law in (Ottoman) Bulgaria 1840s–1890s

1. Introduction

1.1 Chronology and periodization

The paper aims to give an overview of the introduction and application of the first westernized commercial laws in (Ottoman) Bulgaria in the second half of the nineteenth century. It takes as a starting point the establishment of the first specialized commercial courts in the Ottoman Empire in the 1840s and continues its analysis following the secession of the Principality of Bulgaria, due to the fact that the 1850 Commercial Law (1850 CL) remained in force for more than two decades in the new Bulgarian state. The period examined by the paper ends with the introduction of the 1898 Commercial Law (1898 CL) which marked a turning point in Bulgarian commercial law history since it broke the hegemony of the French *Code de commerce* as the main source of inspiration for the state's legal frameworks, the German legal tradition superseding its role from the late 1890s.

1.2 Sources

The source material on the history of commercial law in Bulgaria in the second half of the nineteenth century can generally be divided into several large groups:

- Legislation. For the Ottoman period, the most important sources are the published collections of legislative acts in Ottoman-Turkish, French, Greek, Bulgarian and other languages. The sources from this group contain the legal norms of the period, primarily providing information on new Ottoman legislation and its specific provisions.[1] After the establishment of the Principality of Bulgaria in

1 Kanunname-i ticaret, [Istanbul] 1265 (1849); Code de commerce de l'Empire Ottoman, Constantinople (Istanbul) 1850; Düstur (Birinci tertip), vol. 1–3, [Istanbul] 1289–1293 (1872/3–1876/7); Попов, Стоил: Царски търговски законник, Ruschiuk (Ruse) 1866; *Арнаудов, Христо*: Пълно събрание на държавните закони, устави, наставления и високи заповеди на Османската империя, vol. 1–4, Tsarigrad (Istanbul) 1871–1886; *Νικολαΐδης, Δημήτριος*: Οθωμανικοί Κώδηκες, Constantinople (Istanbul) 1871. *Aristarchi, Grégoire*: Législation ottoman ou Recueil des lois, règlements, ordonnances,

1878, the most important source is the State Gazette: DV *(Държавен вестник: ДВ)*, which published all new laws and regulations as part of the promulgation process.

- Documents created by the judicial institutions (court registers, court decisions and rulings, appeals, subpoenas, correspondence with central and local authorities). For the Ottoman period the two most important archives in which sources of this type can be found are the Oriental Collections of the Bulgarian National Library "St. St. Cyril and Methodius": NLCM–OC *("Колекция Ориенталски сбирки", Национална библиотека "Св. Св. Кирил и Методий": НБКМ–ОС)* and Ottoman Archives of the President of the Turkish Republic's Office in Istanbul: BOA *(T. C. Cumhurbaşkanlığı Devlet Arşivleri Başkanlığı Osmanlı Arşivi).* Court archives for the post-1878 period are kept in the Central State Archive: TsDA *(Централен държавен архив: ЦДА)* in Sofia and its regional departments. Sources of this type provide information on the case law, on the internal court organization and the interactions between judicial institutions and various public and private entities.
- Merchants' and companies' archival collections. The documents contained therein are of a varied nature – correspondence, documents concerning specific legal actions (claims, depositions, court decisions, subpoenas, conciliation agreements, etc.), as well as documents of a general legal nature (contracts, bills of exchange, receipts, correspondence with lawyers, etc.). Their private character could sometimes reveal valuable information that is almost absent in official documents, such as issues related to corruption and patronage, complaints on the slowness of the judicial process and problems with the enforcement of decisions. The main archives for personal documents collections are the Bulgarian Historical Archive in the National Library "St. St. Cyril and Methodius": NLCM–BHA *(Български исторически архив, Национална библиотека "Св. св. Кирил и Методий": НБКМ–БИА)* and the Central State Archive in Sofia, as well as its regional departments.
- Periodicals and newspapers. They provide information on legal and judicial frameworks, debates over the need and the nature of reforms as well as on individual commercial cases.

---

traités, capitulations et autres documents officiels de l'Émpire Ottoman, Constantinople 1873–1881, vol. 1–6; *Young, George*: Corps de droit ottoman: recueil des codes, lois, règlements, ordonnances et actes les plus importants du droit intérieur et d'études sur le droit coutumier de l'Empire Ottoman, Oxford 1905–1906, vol. 1–7.

1.3 The state of research into 1840s–1890s Bulgarian commercial law

Nineteenth-century Bulgarian legal history is a relatively under-researched area in Bulgarian scholarship. Since it is an interdisciplinary topic, research has been done both by historians and legal scholars. The interest is however slightly stronger in legal academic circles, and so far, research has predominantly been authored by jurists rather than historians. There is a noticeable contrast with research on fifteenth to eighteenth century legal and judicial history in Bulgaria, which has traditionally been studied by historians. During the state socialism period, Fani Milkova and Mihail Andreev published overview textbooks on Bulgarian legal history and specialized articles on various aspects of nineteenth century Bulgarian legal history.[2] In the post-1989 period, Ottoman civil proceedings were researched by Nikolai Panayotov.[3] Commercial law in the early decades of the Principality of Bulgaria was partially covered in several overview books on Bulgarian legal history, written primarily by legal scholars teaching university courses on history of Bulgarian law.[4] Until recently, there were almost no publications on the history of commercial law in nineteenth century Bulgaria.[5] To the extent that it exists, research focuses mainly on the development of commercial legal norms and judicial institutions. Whilst problems related to the actual application of the law and the functioning of its institutions are considered in the research, the area remains sorely under-researched. In recent years, there is however an increased interest in the impact of westernized commercial laws on the legal and broader socio-economic

2 *Милкова, Фани/Андреев, Михаил*: История на българската феодална държава и право, Sofia 1993; Андреев, Михаил: История на българската буржоазна държава и право 1878–1917, Sofia 1993; *Milkova, Fanny*: Les traits caractéristiques et l'application du droit civil ottoman dans les terres bulgares au XIXe siècle, Bulgarian Historical Review 1975, no. 4, pp. 26–37; *Milkova, Fanny*: Influence du droit d'Europe occidentale sur le système juridique de Turquie, Bulgarian Historical Review 1982, no. 4, pp. 92–97.

3 *Панайотов, Николай*: Гражданското съдопроизводство в залеза на Османската империя, Varna 1995.

4 *Джамбазов, Ангел*: Правосъдната система на България: 1878–1944, Sofia 1990; *Токушев, Димитър*: История на новобългарската държава и право (1878–1944), Sofia 2008.

5 The only exceptions are two works of Venelin Ganev which cover Bulgarian commercial law development in the broader context of European legal history until 1914: *Ганев, Венелин*: Историческото развитието на търговско право, Годишник на Софийския университет – Юридически факултет, vol. 12 1915/1916 (1921), pp. 1–275; *Ганев, Венелин*: Историческо развитие на несъстоятелността в главните негови моменти, Годишник на Софийския университет – Юридически факултет, vol. 10–11 1913/1914–1914/1915 (1915), pp. 8–216. In the interwar period numerous commentaries and textbooks on commercial law appeared aimed at fulfilling the educational needs of law students and contemporary jurists. Since the 1898 Commercial Law was in force until 1951 (although with numerous amendments and additions) they are also relevant for researching pre-1914 commercial law.

development of (Ottoman) Bulgaria,[6] which insofar as it concerns the Ottoman period is also part of an international trend of increased interest in commercial law in the late Ottoman Empire.[7]

2. Commercial Law in Ottoman Bulgaria (1840–1877)

2.1 Legislative reforms (1840–1877)

2.1.1 Tanzimat legal reforms: Overview

The first sub-period of this overview on the introduction and application of the French *Code de commerce* in Bulgaria roughly coincides with the Tanzimat period in Ottoman history. The Tanzimat was a period of intense change in the legal and judicial system of the Ottoman Empire. The reforms to the law and judiciary had several main objectives. First, they wanted to adapt the legal structures of the Empire to the changed realities of the nineteenth century world. Starting from the eighteenth century, trade and economic interactions with Western Europe had increased

6 *Атанасова, Светла*: Ролята на османското законодателство от средата на XIX век при изграждането на търговско-производствени структури в българските земи, Архив за поселищни проучвания, 2010, no. 1–2, pp. 37–62; *Машева, Ивелина*: Съдебни институции в областта на търговското право във Варна (40-те–70-те години на XIX век), in: Русев, Иван (ed.): Варна, българите и българските градове, Varna 2016, pp. 75–92; *Masheva, Ivelina*: From Islamic Commercial Law to the French Code de Commerce – Oral and Written Evidences in Commercial Trials in Ottoman Bulgaria During the Tanzimat, Rechtskultur – Zeitschrift für Europäische Rechtsgeschichte, vol. 4 (2015), pp. 33–40; *Машева, Ивелина*: Българските търговци и правната регулация на търговско-финансовите отношения в Османската империя (40-те–70-те години на XIX в.), PhD thesis, Sofia University "St. Kliment Ohridski" (2015); *Машева, Ивелина*: Правосъдието в провинцията – Видинският търговски съд в края на 60-те–нач. на 70-те години на XIX век, Балканите – език, история, култура, vol. 4 (2015), pp. 284–293; *Masheva, Ivelina*: Ottoman Commercial Regulations during the Tanzimat period (1839–1877). Legislation Reforms and Their Application in the Town of Rusçuk, Papers of the American Research Center in Sofia, vol. 1 (2014), pp. 120–130; *Цекова, Снежана*: Създаване на новобългарското търговско право, Ius Romanum, 2016, no. 1, pp. 887–900.

7 *Kenanoğlu, Macit*: Ticaret Kanunnamesi ve Mecelle Işığında Osmanlı Ticaret Hukuku, Ankara 2005; *Ade, Mafalda*: Ottoman Commercial Law and Its Application in Aleppo Province (1850–1880), in: Suraiya, Faroqhi/Gilles Veinstein (eds.): Merchants in the Ottoman Empire, Leuven 2008, pp. 243–258; *Ade, Mafalda*: The Ottoman Commercial Tribunal in Damascus and the Use of Testimony and Evidence in Mixed Cases in the 19th Century, Quaderni Storici, vol. 51 (2016), no. 153, pp. 649–672; *Demirci, Akmandar*: Osmanlı Devletinde Taşra Ticaret Mahkemeleri, PhD thesis, Ankara Üniversitesi 2019; *Izmirlioglu, Ahmet*: Ottoman Commercial Tribunals: Closer than Enemies, Farther than Friends, British Journal of Middle Eastern Studies, vol. 45 (2017), no. 5, pp. 1–20; *Rubin, Avi*: Ottoman Nizamiye Courts: Law and Modernity, New York 2011.

progressively, a process some economic historians define as the "incorporation of the Ottoman lands into the world economy".[8] Secondly, they strived to systematize and codify legislation into a comprehensive and coherent body of law. Legislative reform was part of the overarching aim of Tanzimat-era Ottoman statesmen to strengthen imperial control over the provinces as a way to rectify the damaging decentralization policies of the previous century. French legislative, judicial and administrative models were considered particularly suitable for this purpose due to their leaning towards centralized, hierarchical structures. Thirdly, reforms were conceived to address the nationalist and separatist movements of Balkan Christian minorities. The application of new, Western laws in key areas such as commercial and penal law, combined with the introduction of new judicial institutions, was aimed at reducing the differences in the legal status of Muslims and non-Muslims. This, in turn, Ottoman statesmen hoped, would counteract the increasingly strong separatist movements of Balkan Christians. Lastly, Tanzimat reformers strived to make Ottoman law acceptable to Europeans, not only to address Western diplomatic pressure in this regard, but also to gradually abolish the capitulation system and restore full sovereignty in legal and judicial matters.

The course of the legal reforms was not always smooth and straightforward, which often resulted in a heterogeneous and internally contradictory legal framework. Some of the new legislation, such as the Land Code and the Civil Code *(Mecelle)* were based on classical Ottoman and Islamic traditions, while others borrowed heavily from Western (predominantly French) law. The choice between these two approaches depended not only on the nature of the legal field in question, but also on the balance of power between the pro-western reformers and the anti-Western conservative factions of Ottoman elites at the time when the reforms were launched. For instance, the first attempt to pass a new commercial law failed in 1841 due to the temporary predominance of the conservatives, which resulted not only in the rejection of the law, but also in the dismissal of Mustafa Reshid Pasha, the head of the reformist party, from the government. It was not until his return in 1845 that work on new commercial legislation resumed.[9] A similar struggle accompanied the decision as to whether the Empire should adopt the French *Code civil* or to develop an indigenous civil law legislation. However, in 1867 the Grand vizier Ali pasha's proposition to use the *Code civil* in disputes between Muslims and non-Muslims met with severe opposition and, as a result, the Ottoman civil law was codified

8 *Wallerstein, Immanuel/Kasaba, Reşat*: Incorporation into the World Economy: Change in the Structure of the Ottoman Empire, in: Bacqué-Grammont, Jean-Louis/Dumont, Paul (eds.): Économies et sociétés dans l'Empire ottoman (fin du XVIIIe–début du XXe siècle), Paris 1983, pp. 335–354.

9 *Новичев, Арон*: Борьба между реформаторами и консерваторами в период Танзимата (1839–1853), Тюркологический сборник, 1973, p. 88.

on the basis of classical Ottoman legal traditions and Islamic law.[10] The ensuing mixture of western legal borrowing and indigenous Islamic legislation created a modernized and codified legal system, but one that lacked internal cohesion and homogeneity.

2.1.2 1850 Ottoman Commercial Law

After the return of Mustafa Rashid Pasha to Istanbul—especially after 1846, when he was appointed Grand vizier—reforms in the field of commercial law resumed. In 1847 and 1848 the commercial courts were reformed and immediately afterward a commercial code was drafted based on the French *Code de commerce* of 1807/1808. The translation was done by an Ottoman official of Armenian descent, Chamic Ohannes Efendi, but the quality of the translation is criticized by some contemporary Turkish scholars as incorrect and ambiguous.[11] By 1849 the text of the new code was promulgated, but it did not come into force until 1850.[12]

The new commercial code consisted of two parts which corresponded to Part I (On the Commerce in General) and Part III (On Bankruptcy) of the Napoleonic commercial code.[13] The part concerning maritime trade was dismissed as irrelevant for Ottoman purposes. The part on the organization of commercial courts was also omitted, for fear of the possible reaction of the religious class thereto.

2.1.2.1 Company law

The 1850 CL established that merchants were considered business entities under the law and provided the requirements to be met in order to be recognized as such. The definition given in Art. 1 was extremely general in stating that merchants were persons who "carry out trade" and "who make transactions with bills of exchange". The broad definition allowed courts to broaden the scope of application of the commercial law. However, in cases of non-merchants the law was applicable only to the extent that their activity was considered mercantile, i.e. the purchase and sale of goods, use of financial instruments, such as bills of exchange and bankruptcy. This was one of the main points where the Ottoman Law deviated from the French text, which stated that a merchant is a person for whom commerce is "a habitual profession".

---

10 *Шабанов, Фарух*: О светских правовых нормах в законодателстве Османской империи периода реформ XIX в., Тюркологический сборник, 1978, pp. 180–186.

11 *Bozkurt, Gülnihal*: Batı Hukukunun Türkiye'de Benimsenmesi, Ankara 2010, p. 151.

12 Both 1849 and 1850 are used in literature to mark the adoption of the law.

13 *Попов, Стоил*: Царски търговски законник; *Арнаудов, Христо*: op. cit. Hereafter references to the 1850 CL are made using its Bulgarian translation.

The licensing regime for commercial activity under the law was also quite liberal. The requirements for engaging in commercial activity included only reaching a certain age: 21 years. However, persons between the ages of 18 and 21 could still engage in commercial activity, provided that they had the consent of their parents/guardians and a permit from the Ministry of Commerce. Furthermore, with the exception of joint-stock companies, which needed a sultan's decree, the establishment of a business entity did not require a special permit or even registration.

The Commercial Law defined three types of commercial entities:

- *General partnership.* The business entity with the simplest structure, a general partnership consisted of two or more persons acting both as representatives of each other and as mutual guarantors. All partners were fully and jointly liable with their personal property for all the activities of the company. The company's own name had to include the name of at least one of the partners. In general partnership entities profits and losses were distributed among the partners in pre-agreed proportions, depending on the capital and labor that each of them invested in the joint venture.
- *Limited partnership.* Its most important feature was the existence of two types of partners. The first type's rights and obligations were identical to the rights and obligations of the partners in the general partnership. The second type of partners, called limited partners, invested only capital in the enterprise, but did not participate in its management. Such partners had limited liability and incurred losses only up to the amount of the capital invested in the company.
- *Joint-stock company.* Joint-stock companies were also known as "anonymous companies", due to the fact that, unlike joint and limited partnerships, it did not need to include a partner's name. Also, unlike the other two types of companies, joint-stock companies could be managed by outsiders, i.e. by persons who were not shareholders and who did not bear any material liability for the company's losses. The investors in the company were of limited liability, and like limited partners, they only risked the capital they had invested. The lack of collateral (which for the other types of entities was the personal movable and immovable property of the partners) was considered to carry a high risk of fraud. In order to mitigate this potential danger, joint-stock companies were subject to a licensing regime and those wishing to open such a company had to submit their company contracts, and subsequently their statutes for approval from the Ministry of Finance, which in turn referred the matter for final approval by sultanic decree.

The 1850 CL made significant changes to the existing legal framework affecting company law. Prior to the Tanzimat era, the Ottoman legal system had three sources of law: the religious law *(Shari'a)*, the laws promulgated by the sultans *(kanun)* and custom *(örf)*. In the field of commercial regulations however, the main source of law was Shari'a. Formed in the times of the Arabic Caliphate during the Middle

Ages, it remained in use in the Ottoman Empire, including in the territories of present-day Bulgaria, until the early Tanzimat period. Islamic commercial law recognized several types of business associations:

- *Mufawada* partnership. A total partnership, in which all partners invested all their economic assets (dwelling houses excluded), managed and represented the business together and shared the profits (or bore the losses) in equal shares. Each of the partners was considered an agent *(vekil)* and a surety *(kefil)* of the other(s).
- *Inan* partnership. In an *inan* partnership, each of the partners invested only a certain sum of money. The division of the profits (or losses) was agreed on in advance and therefore did not have to be in equal shares. This kind of partnership presumed only agency relations between the partners; they were not mutual guarantors of each other with regard to third parties. The great advantage of the *inan* partnership was its flexibility, since it allowed different combinations of investment and profit-division shares.
- *Mudaraba* partnership. Similar to the Western *commenda*, the *mudaraba* partnership was a partnership in which one party was considered the "investor" and the other the "agent". The capital of the venture was supplied by the investor, but he remained a passive partner. The agent invested the money and gave a certain pre-agreed share of the profits to the investor. After the end of the venture, the original capital was returned to the investor. If there was a loss rather than profit, this was borne solely by the investor.
- *Vücuh*. Also known as the "partnership of the poor", or the "partnership of credit", *vücuh's* purpose was to enable people without financial resources, but who enjoyed a good reputation to obtain capital for a business venture. The distribution of profits in this type of company was a matter of agreement between the parties. Since the concept of interest was a controversial one in Shari'a, this business partnership was also used as an instrument for circumventing limitations on credit and interest.[14]

Islamic law did not conceptualize these kinds of partnerships as legal persons in the modern sense; the partnerships were not legal subjects and liability laid solely with the partners and the partnerships automatically dissolved with the death of a partner. These characteristics of Islamic company law, especially the absence of the

14 *Gerber, Haim*: Muslim Law of Partnerships in Ottoman Court Records, Studia Islamica, vol. 53 (1981), pp. 109–119; *Çizakça, Murat*: Comparative Evolution of Business Partnerships. The Islamic World and Europe with Specific Reference to the Ottoman Archives, Leiden 1996. *Gedikli, Fehti*: Osmanlı Şirket Kültürü: XVI.–XVII. Yüzyıllarda Mudârebe Uygulaması, İstanbul 1998.

concept of corporation, is considered by some authors to have had a great impact on the economic development of Islamic societies.[15]

Of the three types of commercial entities defined by the 1850 CL, only the joint-stock company could be considered a significant legal innovation of the new law. General and limited partnerships were known and utilized by local merchants even before the reform. Moreover, their characteristics could be recreated within the *muwafada* and *inan* Islamic law partnerships. Indeed, we have court decisions from Northern Bulgaria dating from the late 1840s and early 1850s which use mixed terminology defining a business relationship both in the terms of Islamic law and new westernized legal terminology.[16]

In contrast, the joint-stock company was an entirely new concept, both for the Ottoman legal system and for local merchants. Due to its specific characteristics, the joint-stock company had two significant advantages over general partnerships and limited partnerships. The first advantage was its impersonality: the shareholders participating in the company were detached from the day-to-day management process and their shares were easily transferrable. This feature created the potential for stable, long-term existence of joint-stock companies in comparison to the general and the limited partnerships, which, as a rule, discontinued in the event of a partner's death. The second significant feature of joint-stock companies was their ability to raise a large sum of capital within a relatively short period of time. The ownership of the company was divided into small shares, simultaneously significantly expanding the number of potential investors and reducing the potential risk for each investor, as investors were able to diversify their portfolios by investing small and medium amounts into several business ventures.

The 1850 CL regulated the resolution of disputes between partners and the liquidation of companies by requiring that they were first subject to a conciliation procedure. The members of the conciliatory commission were called *mümeyiz*. They were elected by the two disputing parties, or, in the case of disagreement between the parties, appointed ex officio by the commercial court. Only if the commission was unable to reach a decision – or in case one of the two parties was not satisfied with its decision – could the case be transferred to the commercial court. If we compare the new conciliation procedure with pre-existing legal practices, it becomes evident that the new law ultimately changed very little. Prior to the reform individuals highly respected within the local community played a similar role in the process. They established the facts of the case by reviewing the company's documents and

15 *Kuran, Timur*: The Absence of the Corporation in Islamic Law: Origins and Persistence, The American Journal of Comparative Law, vol. 53 (2005), no. 4, pp. 785–834; *Kuran, Timur*: The Long Divergence. How Islamic Law Held Back the Middle East, Princeton 2011.

16 *Masheva, Ivelina*: Ottoman Commercial Regulations during the Tanzimat period (1839–1877), pp. 120–130.

confirmed the authenticity of the evidence presented, on which the court issued its decision. Even after the coming into force of the new code, the resolution of disputes between partners and the liquidation of companies remained the least institutionalized area of commercial law, with the majority of cases resolved through out-of-court mechanisms rather than formal court decisions.

2.1.2.2 Commercial documentation, debt and the concept of interest

Arts. 4–9 of the 1850 CL defined the types of ledgers that each merchant was obliged to keep: (1) daily books with a record of all business transactions, including all bills of exchange that the merchant had drawn, accepted or endorsed; (2) copying books containing all of the letters that the merchant had sent to his business partners; and (3) annual balance sheets. Every year the merchants were required to certify and number their ledgers in the commercial court. This measure was evidently aimed at making ledgers reliable evidence in commercial trials as it reduced the risk of falsification and fraud.

The 1850 CL also regulated in detail the lawful use of financial instruments, most notably of bills of exchange and promissory notes. It stipulated the legal requirements of their form and other mandatory elements; the rules for their endorsement; and, vitally, the procedure to be followed in case of overdue liabilities. Bills of exchange and promissory notes were widely used in the Balkans for centuries, but in the eighteenth and nineteenth centuries, in parallel with an intensification of trade, their use became progressively more widespread. These financial instruments were also not entirely new to the Ottoman and Islamic legal tradition, which indeed had known and used similar tools since the early centuries of the Arab Caliphate (*the hawala* and *suftaja* respectively). Along with the similarities, there were also some differences. The most important of these were the 1850 CL's detailed regulation and penalization of any delayed payments, official regulation of interest rates and, as a consequence of those measures, a greater overall protection of creditors against defaulting debtors.

The legal treatment of interest in cases of delayed repayments was one of the most important changes the 1850 CL introduced in the Ottoman legal system. While interest-bearing loans were utilized and regulated in Islamic jurisprudence *(fiqh)*, legal pronouncements *(fetva)* and sultanic laws *(kanun)* in the Ottoman Empire prior to the adoption of the 1850 Law, the legal treatment of interest was ambiguous. The source of the ambiguity was a text in the Qur'an prohibiting *ribā*, a term which can be translated as "interest", but which had been interpreted by some Islamic jurists to mean "usury", i.e. an *excessive* interest rate. The latter interpretation was the one predominant in nineteenth century Ottoman jurisprudence.[17] Thus, moderate interest rates were considered lawful and were accordingly regulated by the government. In 1852, a sultanic *firman* set a 12% limit (annually) of lawful interest (with the exception of pious foundations and orphans' funds, which were allowed to lend money at a 15% rate and the Istanbul bankers, which were subject to special regulation).[18] In 1864, the *firman* of 1852 was amended; the new text explicitly stated that any document which created an agreement under which interest was to be charged in excess of 1% per month or 12% per annum would be rejected by the commercial courts.[19]

While prior to the 1850 CL interest was accepted within the above-mentioned limits when explicitly negotiated as part of a transaction, it was not an implied consequence of overdue payments. As an example of the changes the 1850 reforms introduced with regard to debt collection and interest, let us consider a decision of the *kadi* court in Ruse. In September 1860, it heard a dispute between Petko, son of Slavcho, and Anderi, son of Momchi, both from Turnovo. Petko commissioned Anderi to receive from Stati Papazoglu 15 spools of cotton silk on his behalf, and to pay for the product with money which he had provided. In court, Petko accused Anderi of having received the goods, but having failed to pay the full price for them, instead, using his money to invest in a different business venture. Petko accordingly asked the court to return the money which he had given to Anderi, with interest added thereto. The judge explicitly ruled that although the practice of paying interest on an overdue payment was contrary to Shari'a, since the case was tried under the Commercial Law, Petko's claim was admissible and the money would be repaid with the accrued interest.[20] This difference between the two legal systems was particularly important in the context of nineteenth century Ottoman economy, due to the common usage of deferred payments, purchases on credit and installed payments in commercial transactions.

2.1.2.3 Rules of procedure, evidence and proof: the 1861 Commercial Procedure Law (CPL)

Another major difference between the Islamic legal system and the later adopted Westernized commercial laws was the procedure rules. First, with regard to evidence and proof, Islamic law recognized three types of evidence – oral testimonies, written evidence and oath. Research on the judicial practice of the Ottoman *kadi* courts confirms that oral testimonies had a primary role in the judicial process. Written

17 *Çağatay, Neşet*: Ribā and Interest Concept and Banking in the Ottoman Empire, Studia Islamica, vol. 32 (1970), pp. 53–68.

18 *Aristarchi, Grégoire*: Législation ottoman, vol. 1, pp. 45–50.

19 Съветник, year 2, issue 3, 6 (18) April 1864.

20 НБКМ–ОС, R 27, p. 64a, doc. 2.

documents were presented less frequently and they were usually accompanied by witness testimonies corroborating their validity.[21] These observations of *kadi* court practice in earlier periods and various Ottoman regions are fully consistent with known *kadi* court practice in Bulgaria. Furthermore, the Islamic law's ideal witness was male, Muslim, and of good repute, which put the testimonies of non-Muslims at a disadvantage. This characteristic of Islamic law was one of the main concerns of Western businessmen operating in the Ottoman Empire, as they considered it not only a discriminatory practice, but also a means through which fraud could be perpetrated through the use of bribed witnesses. The issue was addressed both in the capitulation treaties the Ottoman Empire concluded with foreign powers and the patents *(berats)* issued to privileged non-Muslim Ottoman merchants *(beratlı tüccarları)*.[22] Accordingly, foreign and domestic merchants afforded privileges under the treaties and *berats* had the right to demand court decisions based on written evidence, instead of oral testimonies.[23]

While the reforms did not introduce new types of evidence, they did shift the relative importance of existing types of evidence within the judicial process. Hand-in-hand with the formalization and westernization of business practices, written evidence began to be used with increasing frequency in commercial trials. Documents presented as proof in commercial litigations included bills of exchange, promissory notes, contracts, ledgers, balance sheets and receipts. Oral testimonies were also presented in the course of trials in commercial courts, but they differed from those usually given in *kadi* courts. Generally, it was not third parties but the litigants themselves who gave testimony in commercial courts. Their testimonies were either part of the deposition, explaining certain details pertaining to the matter of the claim, or they testified in their capacity as authors of the presented documents, confirming the authenticity of their content. In both cases however, it was the written document that was essential to the outcome of the case; the oral testimony of the witness had only the supplementary function of verifying and/or clarifying the presented documentation.[24] Under the reformed commercial laws, the role of the oral testimonies decreased significantly, thus reducing the possibility of fraud. Conversely, written documents not only became more widely used, but also much more formalized in their form and content.

---

21 *Ergene, Boğaç*: Evidence in Ottoman Courts of Law: Oral and Written Documentation in Early-Modern Courts of Islamic Law, Journal of American Oriental Society, vol. 124 (2004), pp. 471–491.

22 On the status of *beratlı* merchants see: *Masters, Bruce*: The Sultan's Entrepeneurs: The Avrupa Tüccarıs and the Hayriye Tüccarıs in Syria, International Journal of Middle East Studies, vol. 24 (1992), no. 4, pp. 579–597; *Bağış, Ali*: Osmanlı Ticaretinde Gayri Müslimler. Kapitülasyonlar-Beratlı Avrupa ve Hayriye Tüccarları (1750–1839), Ankara 1983.

23 *Masheva, Ivelina*: From Islamic Commercial Law to the French Code de Commerce, pp. 33–40.

24 Ibid.

A highly formalized procedural framework was introduced to the commercial courts under the 1861 CPL. Each step of every case was regulated in detail and had to meet a number of formal criteria in order to be considered lawful. For instance, during the course of the proceedings, the parties to the case were required to produce and submit a number of specialized legal documents. Some, like the claim itself, had to be written on a special blank *(varaka-i sahihe)*, the cost of which was considered part of the trial's expenses. In addition, most documents submitted in court had to be provided in triplicate – one was to be kept by the party that had produced it, one was given to the opposing party and one was deposited with the court. Even small deviations from the prescribed form of such documents could – and indeed did – lead to their rejection or annulment, which in turn caused significant delays for the affected cases.

Procedural rules of *kadi* courts differed significantly from those contained in the 1861 CPL. Depositions and claims were usually made orally and there were no requirements as to the precise form or language in which claims had to be made. Thus, we can see that the *kadi* courts' procedures were more accessible to various social groups, such as illiterate and poorly educated people or ethnic minorities who did not need any specialized knowledge or experience to represent themselves in court.[25] Although Islamic law recognized the existence of a 'legal representative' for court cases, their role differed significantly from that of a modern lawyer; in *kadi* courts, for example, representatives – often a close relative or friend of the litigant – would represent a litigant unable or unwilling to appear in court.[26]

By contrast, navigating the procedures enacted by the 1861 CPL required education, legal expertise and/or experience in judicial proceedings. This, in turn, stimulated various social changes, most notably the emergence of the modern lawyer in Bulgaria during the 1860s and 1870s. From 1865 onwards, several people from various ethno-religious groups started advertising their legal services in the Дунав/Tuna [Danube] newspaper.[27] Another example was the former clerk of

---

25 *Jennings, Ronald*: Limitations of Judicial Powers of the Kadi in 17th C. Ottoman Kayseri, Studia Islamica, vol. 50 (1978), pp. 180–184.

26 *Jennings, Ronald*: The Office of the Vekil (Wakil) in 17th Century Kayseri, Studia Islamica, vol. 42 (1975), pp. 147–169.

27 Дунав/Tuna, year 1, issue 34, 20 October (1 November) 1865; Дунав/Tuna, year 5, issue 399, 3 (15) August 1869; Дунав/Tuna, year 8, issue 747, 4 (16) February 1873; Дунав/Tuna, year 8, issue 748, 7 (19) February 1873; Дунав/Tuna, year 9, issue 760, 21 March (2 April) 1873; Дунав/Tuna, year 9, issue 761, 25 March (6 April) 1873; Дунав/Tuna, year 9, issue 837, 23 December 1873 (4 January 1874); Дунав/Tuna, year 10, issue 900, 18 (30) August 1874; Дунав/Tuna, year 10, issue 901, 21 August (2 September) 1874; Дунав/Tuna, year 10, issue 902, 25 August (6 September) 1874; Дунав/Tuna, year 10, issue 958, 23 March (4 April) 1875; Дунав/Tuna, year 11, issue 975, 28 May (9 June) 1875; Дунав/Tuna, year 12, issue 1082, 27 June (9 July) 1876; Дунав/Tuna, year 12, issue 1147, 27 February (11 March) 1877.

the Vidin commercial court, Rafat Effendi, who, in 1870, filed for and received the court's approval to practice as a lawyer in the city.[28] In addition to the appearance of lawyers, the complexity of the reforms also encouraged investment in legal education. Merchants, whole communities and various charitable organizations supported students studying law in Western Europe. In the 1860s and 1870s commercial law also started to be taught in various specialized schools within the Ottoman Empire. One of the most popular ones among Bulgarians were Robert College in Istanbul, a secondary school in Plovdiv and the Higher School of Commerce in Svishtov. Finally, the shift to westernized commercial law stimulated the publication of legal educational materials in the Bulgarian language, such as collections of translated Ottoman legal norms, commercial guidebooks and compilations of sample documents (various types of contracts, bills of exchange, promissory notes, legal claims etc.).[29]

2.1.2.4 Bankruptcy

Islamic law treated bankruptcy *(iflâs)* and general debt recovery following a debtor's default in a similar manner. The main legal sanction imposed on a defaulting debtor was the confiscation of property and its forced sale. In addition, this measure could also have been accompanied by the imprisonment of the debtors, which served as both a punishment and as a means to curtail their ability to interfere with the investigation of their finances by hiding and/or selling their property.[30] An illustration of how the issue was handled prior to the adoption of the 1850 CL is the case of *Panayot Keremidchioglu vs. Stati Andrei* from Turnovo. In 1846, Keremidchioglu obtained a court order for the forced sale of Stati Andrei's shop as he was owed 12,500 piasters[31] by him. The real estate was sold for 15,000 ps., which exceeded the amount due to Keremigchioglu. For that reason, a notice to other potential local creditors was to be publicly announced; the excess was to be returned to Stati Andrei if no further creditors came forward.[32]

---

28 НБКМ–ОС, Rs 68/1, p. 4a, doc. 1.

29 *Попов, Стоил*: Царски търговски законник; *Арнаудов, Христо*: op.cit.; *Гранитски, Анастас*: Тръговско ръководство за тръгуване, промишленост, мореплавание и за търговски делания, Tsarigrad (Istanbul) 1858; *Попов, Стоил/Чорапчиев, Иван*: Турско-български писмовник, Ruschiuk (Ruse) 1868.

30 *Tyan, Émile*: Iflâs et procédure d'exécution sur les biens en droit musulman (madhab hanafite), Studia Islamica vol. 21(1964), pp. 145–166; *Atar, Fahrettin*: İflâs, İslam Ansiklopedisi, vol. 21, Istanbul 2000, pp. 511–512.

31 Equivalent to Turkish *kuruş/guruş* and Bulgarian *грош (grosh)*; hereinafter: ps.

32 BOA, A}MKT, D. 54, G. 4.

The 1850 CL's second part, consisting of 132 articles, introduced significant changes to the bankruptcy procedure. The law introduced several significant changes as compared with the prior regulations in Islamic law, namely:

- a special procedure to ensure that creditors were more likely to be informed about the bankruptcy through measures including a public announcement and publication in a local newspaper.
- entrusting the management of the debtor's properties to special trustees, called *syndics* who were required to act both in the interests of the debtor(s) and their creditors. In addition to the trustees, a court official, called a *juge-commissaire,* was also involved in the procedure. The *juge-commissaire* responsibility included supervising and facilitating the bankruptcy proceedings, as well as reporting to the commercial court the development of the case.
- affording creditors collective rights to make binding decisions regarding debt recovery, even without unanimity.
- allowing for review and possibly annulment of transactions made by the debtor before the official bankruptcy date.
- allowing debts to be collected before they reached maturity.
- enabling creditors to enter into an agreement *(concordato)* with the debtor for the deferred payment of a proportion of their debt. Such agreements fixed the amount and terms of the contributions that were to be paid. As a rule, both parties compromised on certain points: creditors wrote off a certain part of their debt as irretrievable and allowed the debtor(s) to continue their business, from the income of which they would gradually repay their debt. For their part, the debtor(s) agreed to pay more than the creditors could otherwise obtain by selling their property.

2.2 Judicial reforms (1840–1877)

2.2.1 Early commercial courts (1840s–1850s)

The reorganization of the Ottoman judicial system started in 1840 with the creation of two new types of courts: the examination councils that judged criminal cases and the commercial councils.[33] The first commercial court was established in Istanbul in 1840 and underwent major reorganizations in 1847 and 1848.[34] From 1847 onwards, a network of commercial councils was gradually established in the big provincial

33 The new institutions were initially not called courts *(mahkeme)*, a term still reserved for the *kadi* courts but rather councils *(meclis)*.

34 *Kenanoğlu, Macit*: op. cit., pp. 25–26.

commercial centers of Izmir, Edirne, Thessaloniki, Cairo and Alexandria. These so-called mixed courts had a limited jurisdiction, primarily regulating disputes between foreigners and Ottomans subjects, as well as disputes involving privileged Ottoman merchants. They were, however, important for two reasons. First, although foreign merchants and privileged Ottoman merchants might not have been as numerous as previously thought,[35] they nevertheless held an important economic position as intermediaries in the international trade between the Ottoman Empire and Western Europe. Consequently, foreigners, foreign protégés and domestic privileged merchants managed vast trade networks, sometimes consisting of several hundred business partners. Furthermore, one of their important privileges was the right to transfer litigations (including disputes with unprivileged merchants) to commercial courts and to transfer their litigation to Istanbul if no such institution was available in town. Secondly, it was in these courts that institutional and normative changes in commercial law were usually first implemented.

Commercial courts started to appear in Ottoman Bulgaria in the early 1850s. Prior to the 1860 reform of the commercial courts, such institutions were established in several Bulgarian cities. So far, we have evidence of the establishment of such institutions in Turnovo (1852), Vidin (prior to 1855), Plovdiv (1856), Varna (1857), Ruse (1858) and Shumen (prior to 1859). Their organization and composition followed closely that of the Istanbul commercial court after the 1848 reorganization. They were composed of a chairman appointed by the government and by representatives of the Muslim *(hayriye tüccarları)* and non-Muslim *(Avrupa tüccarları)* privileged merchants. In case of 'mixed disputes' between foreigners and Ottomans, representatives of foreign nations were invited to sit on the bench, ensuring that composition was equally Ottoman and foreign. The mixed courts settled commercial disputes on the basis of contemporary commercial and business practices, which by that time were strongly westernized.[36]

Prior to the 1860 Supplement of the Commercial Law which reformed the commercial courts system, disputes between Ottoman subjects without a *berat* were tried in the *kadi* court at first instance and in the provincial councils at second instance. De jure after 1850 these institutions tried cases under Ottoman commercial law, rather than Islamic law. However, data on the actual judicial practices of the *kadi* courts is contradictory. On the one hand, we have instances where *kadi* courts applied the new, westernized legislation, rather than Islamic law, such as the above-mentioned case of *Petko, son of Slavcho vs. Anderi, son of Momchi*, in which the *kadi* court based its decision on the 1850 CL, while at the same time explicitly

35 *Boogert, Maurits*: The Capitulations and the Ottoman Legal System. Qadis, Consuls and Beratlıs in the 18th Century, Leiden 2005.

36 *Машева, Ивелина*: Българските търговци и правната регулация на търговско-финансовите отношения в Османската империя.

stating its discrepancy with Islamic law.[37] On the other hand, however, *kadi* courts seemed to have continued to apply Islamic law instead of the new legislation in other instances. The case between Dimitraki, a *beratlı* merchant from Nish, and 19 peasants from the districts of Vidin, Belogradchik and Lom is an excellent example in this regard. In December 1851 they concluded a contract for the supply of 20,000 okkas of wool to the merchant by 20 May 1852. In case the peasants failed to deliver the wool, they were obliged to pay, as compensation, the price of the wool at Istanbul market prices; this, at 5 ps. per okka, amounted to a sum of 120,000 ps., for which they also became mutual guarantors. Neither the wool nor the compensatory sum was delivered and so Dimitraki filed a lawsuit in the Vidin *kadi* court. In the course of the case, however, the peasants made a counteraccusation, claiming that this was in fact not a purchase contract but a case of usury. According to the defendants, Dimitraki had given them a loan of 50,000 ps. at a difficult time. They had a receipt for the funds received and wished to repay the merchant, together with the interest and expenses that he had incurred (amounting to 15,000 ps.) for a total of 65,000 ps. The *kadi* court ruled that these 65,000 ps. undoubtedly belonged to Dimitraki, but that the rest of the amount up to 120,000 ps. could not to be collected without a court decision. The case was subsequently referred to the Vidin council as a second instance, but that court also failed to find a solution, satisfying Dimitraki. The council's position largely reiterated that of the *kadi* court and both judicial institutions were reluctant to award the entire sum of 120,000 ps. to the merchant.[38] Although, according to the 1850 CL the contract was legal, the courts did not rule in Dimitraki's favor; instead, they only accepted the merchant's claim for 50,000 ps. as indisputable, as well as its accompanying costs and accrued interest. In this way, they took the side of the peasants who claimed that this was a matter of usury and not a contract of sale. Their decision seems to be strongly influenced by Islamic legal tradition, according to which both the future purchase of agricultural products *(selem)* and loans with high interest rates *(ribā)* were quite controversial from a legal point of view. The already mentioned 1852 regulation, which fixed the upper limit of any borrowing to a 12% annual rate, might have also influenced the decision of the local judicial institutions. While the regulation explicitly included *selem* contracts, it exempted such contracts that had been concluded before the regulation came into force. However, it seems that in Dimitraki's case local courts were reluctant to do so even though the contract was concluded in December 1851 and the loan was accordingly not subject to the 12% interest limit.[39] The case is

37 НБКМ–ОС, R 27, p. 64a, doc. 2.

38 BOA, HR.MKT, D. 62, G. 94.

39 *Özdeğer, Mehtap/Zeytinli, Emine*: Ottoman Credit System and Usurers in Agriculture in the Nineteenth Century: Practices of Usury Contracts (Selem), Journal of Balkan and Near Eastern Studies, vol. 21 (2018), no. 5, pp. 594–612.

indicative of the complexities of a heterogeneous legal system in which the norms of the commercial law as well as of civil law in general were derived from different, and sometimes contradictory, legal traditions.

Unfortunately, the final outcome of the case is unknown, as the archival folder's does not include any information past Dimitraki's request to transfer the case to the Istanbul Commercial Court, where he apparently hoped to receive a more favorable decision. This brings to the fore another important aspect of the Ottoman legal and judicial system of the 1840s and 1850s: the existence of privileged merchant classes. Two special categories of merchants existed, the members of which enjoyed differential legal treatment compared with ordinary tradesman. This approach created a framework in which legal pluralism could develop; the right of foreigners and *beratlı* merchants to transfer their cases from provincial *kadi* and local courts to commercial courts, including to Istanbul if a local commercial court did not exist, created distinct opportunities for 'forum shopping'. A look at the BOA archives in Istanbul reveals that, in the 1840s and 1850s, Dimitraki's case was far from an isolated instance. The archive contains hundreds, if not thousands, of requests from various privileged merchants to transfer their cases to the Istanbul Commercial Court, which points to the conclusion that the foreign and *beratlı* merchants' privilege to request a court transfer for their case gave them a significant advantage in legal conflicts.

2.2.2 Commercial courts in the 1860s and 1870s

In 1856 the Reform Edict *(Islahat Hatt-ı Hümayunu)* was promulgated by the Sultan. Among other important reforms, it promised that the penal and commercial law, as well as the procedure law for the new secular courts, would be codified as soon as possible. Consequently, in the early 1860s, three new commercial codes were passed and they were all again modeled after French Napoleonic codes. First, in 1860, a Supplement of the Commercial Law (SCL) regulating the organization of the commercial courts was passed, followed by the Commercial Procedure Law in 1861 and the Law on Maritime Commerce in 1863.[40]

2.2.2.1 1860 Supplement of the Commercial Law: Structure and composition of the new commercial courts

The 1860 SCL regulated in detail the structure and composition of the courts. The new commercial courts were composed of a chairman, two permanent members and two further provisional members. The chairman and the permanent members were nominated by the local administrative authorities and formally appointed

---

40 *Попов, Стоил*: Царски търговски законник.

by the central government. They had the status of paid civil servants and could hold their position for an unlimited time. Unlike them, the provisional members were elected by the local merchant community; they worked pro bono and were limited to two one-year terms. In practice, however, the term limits were not strictly enforced, and some provisional members were known to have served for longer.[41] To be eligible to serve as a provisional member, one had to be a merchant with at least five years of professional commercial experience and be at least 30 years old. In addition, they must not have previously been bankrupt (or if they did, they had subsequently been restored all their rights) and needed a clean criminal record.

While not stated in the 1860 SCL, sources reveal that, in many instances, the local ethno-religious balance was also taken into account during the recruitment process. The names of the Vidin commercial court's personnel from 1285 AH (1868) to 1294 AH (1877) reveal that there was always one Muslim and one non-Muslim permanent member on the court. Two of the provisional members were always Muslims, while the other two were non-Muslims, the positions usually divided between Christians and Jews.[42] Another model of local ethno-religious balancing which influenced the appointment process to the courts could be observed in Plovdiv. At the end of 1863, the provincial governor nominated two of the city's notables, Arif Ağa and H. Süleyman Ağa, to become the chairman and a permanent member, respectively, of the city's commercial court.[43] The other members of the court (one permanent and four temporary members) were elected by a council of 25 merchants, composed of five members from each of the five main local communities: the Turks, Bulgarians, Greeks, Armenians and Jews. They chose one merchant from each community and subsequently selected at random who would be the permanent member. The other four were appointed as provisional members.[44]

2.2.2.2 Commercial courts in the Ottoman judicial system: Hierarchy and jurisdiction

According to the 1860 SCL on the organization of the courts, decisions issued by the commercial courts of first instance were subject to appeal to the Istanbul Commercial Court. In 1864, the Law on the Organization of the Danube Province *(Tuna Vilâyeti Nizâmnâmesi)* and the Provincial Reform Law *(Vilâyet Nizamnâmesi)*,

---

41 Salname-i Vilâyet-i Tuna: vol. 1–10, [Ruscuk] 1285–1294 (1868–1877).

42 Salname-i Vilâyet-i Tuna: vol. 1–10, [Ruscuk] 1285–1294 (1868–1877); cf.: *Saracoglu, Mehmet Safa*: Letters from Vidin: A Study of Ottoman Governmentality and Politics of Local Administration, 1864–1877, PhD thesis, Ohio University, 2007, p. 211.

43 Both were obviously important figures in Plovdiv society. Arif ağa was described as a local notable *(Filibe vucuhundan)*, who also held an honorary post in the imperial stables, while H. Süleyman ağa was the leader *(şehbender)* of the local Muslim *beratlı* merchants *(hayriye tuccarları)* and also held an office as chief of the guard *(kapucu başı)* in the sultan's retinue *(rikâb-ı humayün)*.

44 BOA, I.MVL, D. 508, G. 22959, p. 1–7.

established courts of appeal in the provincial capitals. In accordance with these regulations, a commercial court of appeal was established in Ruse in the mid-1860s. Its first chairman, a Bulgarian named Yanko Effendi, had previously worked in the Istanbul Commercial Court.[45] Later, similar courts were established in other provincial centers. Appeals against the decisions of the courts of first instance had to be made within 121 days of the date on which the judgment was handed down, but, if the person was in the Arab provinces of the empire or in a foreign country, this period was extended to 180, 240 or 360 days, depending on the distance.[46]

The policy regarding the creation of a hierarchical system of commercial courts was aimed at establishing uniform and consistent judicial treatment based on the new laws throughout the Empire. The sustained efforts towards centralization and modernization are well illustrated by the numerous instructions on various matters that the Ministry of Commerce[47] sent to the Vidin commercial court in 1873. They included orders not to change the decisions and rulings of other courts; not to interfere in cassation and appellate proceedings at a higher instance; not to issue decisions and opinions on abbreviated or incomplete evidence, on the basis that they would inevitably be appealed; and, in case of doubts surrounding the meaning of the law, that the practice of the Istanbul Commercial Court or current commercial practices should be considered.[48]

The jurisdiction of the commercial courts was regulated in Articles 27–38 of the 1860 SCL. First and foremost, they tried 'proper' commercial disputes, i.e. those related to the purchasing and sale of goods, the transport of goods by land and sea, the dissolution of commercial companies, commercial representation and bankruptcies. They were also competent to rule on cases involving financial instruments, such as promissory notes, bills of exchange etc. In the jurisdiction of commercial courts were also conflicts related to money exchange *(saraflık)*, banking and bankruptcy. Despite this relatively clear jurisdiction, there were confusions and conflicts between commercial courts and other judicial institutions. Some of those conflicts resulted in complaints to the central government whereas others lead to cases being transferred to other judicial bodies.

In the early 1860s, the main conflict area concerned the separation of powers between commercial courts and *kadi* courts. In September 1861, the Ruse *kadi*

45 BOA, A}MKT.MHM, D. 315, G. 97; Дунав/Tuna, year 1, issue 12, 19 (31) May 1865.

46 *Попов, Стоил*: Царски търговски законник, p. 6.

47 Ministry of Commerce administered the system of the commercial courts from 1840 until 1875 when they were transferred to the newly established Ministry of Justice.

48 НБКМ–ОС, Vd 1/124, see also *Андреев, Стефан/Велков, Аспарух/Груевски, Петко/Иванова, Светлана/Михайлова-Мръвкарова, Мария/Робев, Никола/Силянова, Емилия*: Опис на османотурски документи за занаяти и търговия (XVI–XIX в.), запазени в Ориенталския отдел на Народната библиотека "Св. св. Кирил и Методий", Sofia 1993, p. 429.

court judge *(naib)* sent a complaint to the Sublime Porte, claiming that the city's commercial court was hearing Shari'a lawsuits which should have been heard in the *kadi* court. The complaint was accompanied by a *fetva* in favor of the claim.[49] Turning to the practice of the Ruse *kadi* court, however, we can see that it also tried cases outside its jurisdiction. In June 1864, the Ruse *kadi* court administered bankruptcy proceedings against Netso, son of Dimitri Kantardzioglu, despite the fact that the Ruse commercial court, which had explicit jurisdiction over such proceedings, had been founded six years prior.[50]

In the 1860s and 1870s, commercial courts were occasionally in conflict with the jurisdiction of the administrative councils *(idare meclisleri)*. For example, cases concerning tax farming were to be judged by the administrative councils. However, merchants often combined tax farming with commerce, money lending and other activities, therefore such cases were occasionally filed in the commercial courts by association. Such a case between the Vidin resident George and H. Iako Ventura was initially heard by the Vidin commercial court and subsequently appealed to the Provincial Commercial Court of Appeal. However, the second instance court ruled that the case should not have been tried in a commercial court in the first place, annulled the decision of the Vidin commercial court and transferred the case to the Vidin administrative council.[51]

The new regular civil *(nizamiye)* courts established after 1864 were another judicial institution with which commercial courts had a complicated relationship. The 1860 SCL, as well as later reform legislation, permitted commercial cases to be heard in civil courts, provided that there was no commercial court operating in the town. If a commercial court had been founded, there should not have been, in theory, any conflicts of jurisdiction between the two institutions but, in practice, it seems that matters were much less clear. Let us examine one such case, chosen because it also gives us a glimpse of the non-legal considerations parties took into account in their decision to choose to bring their case before one judicial institution. The case, published in a questionnaire on the functioning of the judicial system in Northern Bulgaria by Prof. Bogišič in 1877, describes an interesting tale of forum shopping and bribery. A financial dispute between local citizens was initially filed and tried in the Vidin commercial court. After the trial, however, it was subsequently brought by the losing party to be retried in the regular civil court. The court, which was presided over by a *kadi* (who, according to the source, had

49 BOA, A} MKT.MHM, D. 234, G. 36.

50 *Masheva, Ivelina*: Ottoman Commercial Regulations during the Tanzimat period (1839–1877), pp. 120–130.

51 Дунав/Tuna, year 9, issue 759, 18 (30) March 1873.

been bribed), decided the case on the basis of testimonies under oath, rather than on written evidence and thus reversed the decision of the commercial court.[52]

2.2.2.3 *Territorial distribution*

Provisional statistical yearbooks from the late 1860s and early 1870s provide information on all judicial institutions in their respective provinces, including commercial courts. The first yearbook of the Danube *vilayet*, published in 1285 AH (1868), lists 13 such judicial institutions in the province – the Provincial Commercial Appeal Court in Ruse and the first instance courts in Silistra, Shumen, Svishtov, Sofia, Tulcea (nowadays in Romania), Constanța (also nowadays in Romania), Turnovo, Niš (nowadays in Serbia), Vidin, Lom, Varna and Balchik.[53] The first yearbook of the Edirne province, published in 1287 AH (1870–1871) lists six commercial courts, of which two (Plovdiv and Sliven) were located in Bulgaria.[54] Between 1868 and the beginning of the Russo-Ottoman War in 1877, the number of commercial courts in Bulgaria had reached 16 (see Map 1).

---

52 *Петров, Петър*: Анкета за дейността на казалийските съдилища Известия на Българското историческо дружество, vol. 37 (1985,), p. 452.

53 Salname-i Vilâyet-i Tuna, vol. 1, 1285 (1868).

54 Salname-i Vilâyet-i Edirne, vol 1, [Edirne] 1287 (1870).

Map 1 Commercial courts in Bulgaria on the eve of the Russo-Ottoman War (1877–1878)[55]

2.2.2.4 *Quantitative data*

In 1870, the Ottoman authorities compiled statistics on some of the more important indicators of the activity of the commercial courts in the empire. The statistics reflected the activity of the courts for one calendar year – 1285, according to the Rumi calendar, corresponding to March 1869 to March 1870 of the Gregorian calendar. Unfortunately, information only exists for ten out of the twelve courts which existed in the territory of present-day Bulgaria. For unknown reasons, the courts in Lom and Shvishtov were not included in the survey, which makes the data only an approximate picture of the activities of the commercial courts in Ottoman Bulgaria.

55 Salname-i Vilâyet-i Tuna, vol. 10, 1294 (1877); Salname-i Vilâyet-i Edirne, vol. 6, 1292 (1875).

Table 1 Statistical data on the number of commercial disputes in Ottoman Bulgaria (1285)[56]

Court	Number of ongoing cases		
	Total number of ongoing cases for the year (including those filed in the previous year)	Cases finished during the year	Cases still ongoing in the end of the year
Varna	237 (1)	132	105
Vidin	207 (7)	133	74
Ruse	207 (91)	137	70
Shumen	170 (0)	166	4
Balchik	157 (0)	134	23
Turnovo	58 (5)	43	15
Sofia	42 (4)	38	4
Silistra	32 (0)	16	16
Plovdiv	113 (6)	40	73
Sliven	87 (1)	34	53
TOTAL	1 310 (115)	873	437

If we compare the data on the commercial courts in Bulgaria with those in other regions of the Empire, we can see that their workload was relatively light. The court with the most cases filed during the year, Varna, was only the eleventh busiest commercial court in the Empire, far behind courts, such as Chania (in Crete) with 701 cases, Baghdad with 673, Damascus with 622, Izmir with 522 and Aleppo with 513 cases. However, one must also take into account the fact that the institutional network was not evenly distributed in all parts of the Empire. By 1870, the Danube *vilayet*, with its 14 judicial institutions, had a very high number of commercial courts and the Edirne *vilayet* was also relatively well covered by a network of seven commercial courts. By comparison, many provinces of the Empire, such as the Balkan provinces of Shkodra, Prizren and Bosnia, only had one commercial court, located in their provincial capital.

56 BOA, T.MAT, D. 792, G. 32, sf. *Kenanoğlu, Macit*: op. cit., pp. 150–220.

Table 2 Sum of the claims and the decisions (1285, in piasters)[57]

Court	Sum of the monetary value claimed in cases before the court	Sum of the monetary value awarded by the court
Varna	1 339 310	1 179 588
Vidin	1 240 796	618 881
Ruse	1 054 870	659 322
Shumen	376 508	360 331
Balchik	486 548	415 297
Turnovo	289 887	225 460
Sofia	340 602	276 174
Silistra	49 386	49 386
Plovdiv	1 072 574	648 252
Sliven	769 258	223 359
TOTAL	5 657 278	3 476 462
Average per court	565 728	347 646

Considering the average number of court rulings in Table 1 with the average sum awarded by the court in Table 2, we can see that the average award of a commercial court in Ottoman Bulgaria was 3,982 ps. The sum was relatively high,[58] which shows that the commercial courts tried disputes with a relatively large financial stake, while disputes over small amounts of money were more likely to be settled by the regular *(nizamiye)* and *kadi* courts.[59]

57 BOA, T.MAT, D. 792, G. 32, sf. *Kenanoğlu, Macit*: op. cit., pp. 150–220.

58 For comparison, the average price of urban real estate in the Danube province according to the 1866 census was 3087,8 ps.; see *Тодоров, Николай*: Балканският град XV–XIX век, Sofia 1972, p. 407.

59 For comparison I can point out an excerpt from the cases tried in the kadi and regular (nizamiye) court of Vidin for Nissan 1283 (13 April–12 May 1867), in which the overwhelming majority of contested sums were below 1,000 ps.: НБКМ-ОС, Vd 4/7.

Table 3 Profile of the cases according to the outcome of the case (1285)[60]

Court	Cases held in favor of the plaintiff	Cases held in favor of the defendant	Cases transferred to a different court	Cases ended by agreement between the parties	Total number of cases
Varna	121	7	2	2	132
Vidin	55	52	9	17	133
Ruse	75	14	43	5	137
Shumen	120	17	23	6	166
Balchik	123	4	-	7	134
Turnovo	31	-	7	5	43
Sofia	30	2	4	2	38
Silistra	16	-	-	-	16
Plovdiv	40	-	-	-	40
Sliven	21	5	8	-	34
TOTAL	632	101	96	44	873
As percentage	72,39	11,57	11,00	5,04	100%

The vast majority of cases – 632 out of 873, or 72,4% of all of the disputes filed – were won by the claimant. By contrast, the cases won by the defendant represented only 11,6% of the total number of cases. There are several factors that could explain the disproportion. First, the cases brought before the courts do not constitute a random sample of all commercial disagreements.[61] The decision to file a lawsuit was made by the plaintiff based on rational assessment of their chances of winning; hence, they would be inclined to go to court only if they felt that the chance to win was high enough to justify the investment of time and money. Therefore, one of the main reasons for the high percentage of lawsuits won by the plaintiff could be the tendency of local merchants to avoid the risks connected with pursuing a long and expensive lawsuit that they weren't likely to win. However, other factors could also affect the outcome of the statistics. One of them was the different stakes that each party had in winning and losing. In cases of delayed payments, which were some of the most common cases to be heard before the commercial court, the creditor was interested in recovering the amounts due as soon as possible, so that they could invest them in other business ventures. By contrast, for the debtor, it might be more profitable to lose a case in court and pay the accrued interest

60 BOA, T.MAT, D. 792, G. 32, sf. *Kenanoğlu, Macit*: op. cit., pp. 150–220.

61 *Priest, George/Klein, Benjamin*: The Selection of Disputes for Litigation. Journal of Legal Studies, vol. 13 (1984), no. 1, pp. 1–55; *Kessler, Daniel/Meites, Thomas/Miller, Geoffrey*: Explaining Deviations from the Fifty-Percent Rule: A Multimodal Approach to the Selection of Cases for Litigation, Journal of Legal Studies, vol. 25 (1996), no. 1, pp. 233–259.

instead of paying the money on time. This is illustrated very clearly in the dispute that Todor Iliev of Svishtov had with a local Armenian merchant in November 1859. In correspondence discussing his intention to file a lawsuit, Iliev complained that his trading partner had chosen to invest in a livestock venture, rather than paying a sum owed to him.[62] If the profit margins of such a venture were higher than the official interest rate, a debtor could turn a profit by waiting for the returns of their investment and then paying back a smaller sum to the creditor on the orders of the court. Thus, losing a case in court could sometimes be a part of the defendant's calculated business strategy, rather than a 'proper' legal dispute which required a genuine defense. The third main factor that explains the huge difference in the proportion of cases won by the plaintiff and the defendant is their different socio-economic position. Small and medium-sized enterprises were in a much more vulnerable financial position compared with large merchant ventures since their activity was rarely diversified enough to mitigate the consequences of a bad deal and/or the bankruptcy of a major business partner. If we take the example of Hristo Tupchileshtov,[63] an affluent Bulgarian merchant who lived in Istanbul, we can see that, in the numerous commercial disputes he had with various Balkan merchants in the 1850s, 1860s, and 1870s, he was almost without exception the claimant, rather than the defendant. His position as a big business owner with a vast domestic and international trade network offered him distinct advantages. First, his expertise in commercial law matters was distinctly greater than that of many of his smaller trading partners from the Ottoman Balkans who often turned to him for advice.[64] Secondly, the scope of his business allowed him to hire a native Turkish-speaking clerk whose tasks most likely included correspondence with various Ottoman administrative, financial and judicial institutions. Thirdly, wealthy merchants of Tupchileshtov's caliber were well connected with the Ottoman central and provincial administrations; for instance, Tupchileshtov had previously been appointed to the Istanbul Commercial Court as an examining clerk *(mümeyiz)* in the dissolution of the partnership between Nikoli Minchooglu and Kostaki Marinchovich.[65] His close connections with members of the Istanbul Commercial Court and the Ministry of Commerce are also evidenced by a letter he wrote to his son Petko in London in 1871. Petko was unsure as to what he should pursue as his

62 НБКМ–БИА, fund (hereinafter: F.) 6, archival entity (hereinafter: a.e.), IA 1916.

63 Hristo Tupchileshtov's archive consisting of tens of thousands of documents is kept in the NLCM and in the Central State Archive. Many documents pertaining to various litigations in which he was a side could also be found in the Ottoman Archive (BOA) in Istanbul; for more information on his life and commercial activities see: *Davidova, Evguenia*: Balkan Transitions to Modernity and Nation-States: Through the Eyes of Three Generations of Merchants (1780s–1890s), Leiden 2012.

64 НБКМ–БИА, F. 6, a.e. IA 412.

65 НБКМ–БИА, F. 6, a.e. IA 8985, p. 344.

major. His father tried to influence him towards commercial law over engineering by mentioning that he could help him advance his career, due to his connections in the commercial legal world. However, if Petko chose engineering, so the letter tells us, his father would have been unable to assist with his career, as he knew no high ranked officials to whom he could recommend him.[66] In 1874 Tupchileshtov also employed his connections to influence the decision from the Ruse commercial court by illegal means. Tupchileshtov traveled to Ruse with the sole purpose of settling litigation with an "Arab merchant". He met with the president of the Ruse court and managed to win him over to his side, but that was not enough, since the other members of the court were still undecided. Eventually, following the bribing of the court member Ibrahim Effendi with a payment of 100 liras, Tupchileshtov managed to secure a favorable outcome for his case.[67]

Table 4 Decisions according to the nationality of the parties (1285)[68]

Court	Cases between Ottoman subjects	Mixed cases between Ottoman and non-Ottoman subjects	Total number of cases
Varna	116	16	132
Vidin	130	3	133
Ruse	123	14	137
Shumen	153	13	166
Balchik	94	40	134
Turnovo	42	1	43
Sofia	36	2	38
Silistra	16	0	16
Plovdiv	27	13	40
Sliven	31	3	34
TOTAL	768	105	873
As percentage	87,97%	12,03%	100%

According to this data, commercial courts in Ottoman Bulgaria dealt mainly with cases involving merchants of Ottoman nationality. Disputes between Ottoman and foreign nationals were just over 12% of the courts' workload. Despite the fact that commercial law reform could be largely attributed to increased trade with Western Europe and western diplomatic pressure, in the 1870s, commercial courts at least in Bulgaria, primarily served the local commercial community, rather than

66 *Davidova, Evguenia*: op. cit., p. 85.
67 НБКМ–БИА, Ғ. 6, a.e. I A 9000, p. 481.
68 *Kenanoğlu, Macit*: op. cit., pp. 181–187.

foreign merchants. Although this official survey does not include data on the ethno-religious background of the Ottoman subjects addressing the court, other sources such as the partially-preserved register of the Vidin commercial court, point to the conclusion that commercial courts were used by all major ethno-religious groups in the region, including Muslims, Orthodox Christians, Jews and Armenians.[69]

Ottoman commercial courts underwent significant evolution during the Tanzimat reforms. In the 1840s and 1850s, access to these new judicial institutions was limited to foreign citizens, foreign protégés and Ottoman *beratlı* merchants. The reforms in the early 1860s made significant changes to their institutional development, universal access to the courts was afforded to all categories of merchants, new rules on the composition and structure of the courts were enacted and procedural rules were codified. By the end of the Ottoman rule, commercial courts had become the main institutions adjudicating commercial and financial litigation in Bulgaria. Statistical data from the 1870s points to the conclusion that there was a dense network of specialized judicial institutions that judged a significant number of cases contesting relatively large sums of money. By the end of the Ottoman rule, commercial courts in Bulgaria were primarily serving the needs of local merchants, craftsmen and other professionals, rather than those of foreigners.

3. Commercial law in the Principality of Bulgaria (1877–1890s)

3.1 Reforms in the judicial system (1877–1890s)

3.1.1 Provisional Russian Administration (1877–1879)

During the Russo-Ottoman War (1877–1878) and its immediate aftermath most of the territory of present-day Bulgaria was governed by an imperial commissary appointed by the Russian emperor. The Russian administration made no substantial changes to the normative or judicial aspects of the antecedent commercial law in force in Bulgaria. In August 1878 it passed the Provisional Rules on the Organization of the Judiciary in Bulgaria *(Временни правила за устройството на съдебната част в България)*. The new rules were modeled after the 1864 Russian Statute for Judicial Institutions but, at the same time, the Provisional Rules tried to preserve existing institutions wherever possible. Accordingly, commercial courts continued

69 *Машева, Ивелина*: Правосъдието в провинцията, p. 290.

to try commercial cases according to the 1850 CL and established commercial practice under Art. 75 of the Provisional Rules.[70]

Although the existence of commercial courts system as a separate institution continued, it is unclear whether all commercial courts continued to exist, or whether it was those in the largest commercial centers that were left preserved. The remaining commercial courts continued to be constituted according to the 1860 SCL, i.e. with a chairman, two permanent and four provisional members. In judicial districts where there was no commercial court, commercial disputes were tried by the regular civil courts. Commercial courts, as well as regional civil courts, could, under Art. 76 of the Provisional Rules, make non-appealable rulings in commercial cases concerning claims of up to 1,000 ps. Cases concerning higher amounts were appealable before the district courts within two weeks following the first instance court decision. Such an appeal was to be filed in the court whose decision was being appealed, which in turn transferred it to the higher instance court, together with the case's documentation. The second instance court had three days to notify the opposing party, who was given two weeks in which to object to the appeal. The opposing party also had the right to object to the appeal during the trial at second instance too.

Commercial cases were initiated by the plaintiff with either a written or an oral claim. The oral claim had to be presented to one of the court members, who wrote it down in a special register. After that, the judge read the transcription of the oral plea to the plaintiff, who had to sign it. Both written and oral claims had to conform to certain rules under Art. 103 of the Provisional Rules. For example, the claim had to be filed in the court of the defendant's domicile. If there was more than one defendant, the plaintiff could choose in which of the defendants' domiciles the claim was filed.[71]

3.1.2 Eastern Rumelia (1878–1885)

Under the Treaty of Berlin (1878) most of Southern Bulgaria (the districts of Plovdiv, Pazardzhik, Sliven, Stara Zagora, Haskovo and Burgas) formed the autonomous province of Eastern Rumelia. It was governed according to the Organic Statute passed in April 1879. As an autonomous territory within the Ottoman Empire, Eastern Rumelia continued to apply Ottoman legislation, including the 1850 CL. The province had its own court system, which consisted of first instance regional courts, second instance district courts and a Supreme Court. Commercial cases

70 *Габровски, М.*: Организация на съдебната власт в България, in: 60 години българско правосъдие (1878–1941), Sofia 1941, pp. 73–121.

71 *Джамбазов, Ангел*: op. cit., pp. 15–43.

were tried at first instance in the regional courts which normally consisted of three judges appointed for life by the government. When trying commercial cases, a jury of two people was summoned to assist the court. The jurors' votes carried the same weight as those of the judges. The General Assembly of Eastern Rumelia elected annually two groups of jurors from the local merchant and business community, each serving for a term of 6 months.[72] These regulations were in force until the unification of Eastern Rumelia with the Principality of Bulgaria in 1885.

3.1.3 The judicial system in the Principality of Bulgaria (1878–1890s)

3.1.3.1 1880 Law on the Organization of the Courts in the Principality of Bulgaria

In 1880 a new Law on the Organization of the Courts *(Закон за устройство на съдилищата)* in the Principality of Bulgaria was passed based on the 1864 Russian Statute for Judicial Institutions. It was followed in 1891 by a Law on Civil Judicial Proceedings *(Закон за гражданското съдопроизводство)* which supplemented some of its provisions. The new organization of the judiciary dispensed with the specialized commercial courts system with its specific organizational and procedural rules. According to the 1880 Law, commercial cases were to be tried in courts' civil sections following the rules and regulations governing civil trials. Generally, the Law did not differentiate between commercial and other civil cases, although there were some exceptions. For example, ledgers and other internal commercial documentation were only accepted as proof without qualification in disputes between merchants. When the decision was not based on the 1850 Commercial Law, litigants' internal documents were accepted as proof in court only in a limited number of cases.

The 1880 Law established the following system of hierarchical judicial institutions:

- *Justices of the peace:* A position occupied by a single judge appointed by the government. They tried civil and commercial cases worth fewer than 1,000 franks (later changed to 1,000 lev), as well as all cases in which the parties had agreed to have their case heard by a justice of the peace. The decisions of the justices of the peace were appealable before the district courts.
- *District courts:* District courts were established in every district center of Bulgaria and were divided into four categories according to the size of the city in which the court sat and the workload of the court. In 1880, for the first time, the district courts were divided into civil and criminal sections, with commercial

72 *Манолова, Мария*: Съдоустройствена система на Източна Румелия, Годишник на Софийския университет – Юридически факултет, vol. 66 (1975), pp. 43–55; *Джамбазов, Ангел*: op. cit., pp. 43–52.

cases being subject to the jurisdiction of the civil section. Unlike in Eastern Rumelia, no jurors took part in commercial trials. The only deviation from the standard rules of civil procedure concerned bankruptcy cases, where an opinion of the public prosecutor was needed in order to rule out fraudulent bankruptcy.

- *Courts of Appeal:* These courts had jurisdiction over the judgments of the district courts at second instance.
- *Supreme Court of Cassation:* The Supreme Court had a dual role in the judicial system. First, it served as the third and final instance court of appeals from the district courts and courts of appeal. Secondly, it also served as an interpreter of the law, setting precedents and filling lacunas in the law. An example of this role was the Court's decision defining the limits of the competences granted to the general assembly of joint-stock companies. According to the Supreme Court, when a decision of a general assembly would be harmful to public order and contradicts the basic principles of the joint-stock company, it was null and void. This conclusion was reached in a case which concerned a dispute on the lawfulness of a general assembly's decision to consider shares not registered by the shareholders within a set time limit as invalid.[73]

3.1.3.2 The 1899 Law on the Organization of the Courts

In 1899 a new Law on the Organization of the Courts *(Закон за устройство на съдилищата)* was passed. It did not make significant changes to the judicial structure but introduced new regulations on the selection and the appointment of judicial personnel. The most important changes enacted included the introduction of a requirement for judges to hold a law degree and the stipulation that certain categories of judges could not be freely removed. Other measures included the introduction of the position of judiciary candidate, a form of internship in which a future court official could gain experience for a period of six to twelve months prior to their appointment to a regular court position. The changes were aimed at improving the judiciary's legal expertise and at limiting the government's ability to influence the court.[74]

The new requirement that judges needed to have a law degree reflected the overall progress in legal education in Bulgaria. The idea was not new but had not yet been implemented due to practical considerations. Until the end of the nineteenth century there were simply not enough people with a law degree in Bulgaria to fill all the judgeship positions. In 1892 however, the newly founded Sofia University established a Faculty of Law. In the first academic year (1892/1893)

---

73 *Джамбазов, Ангел*: op. cit., pp. 52–72; *Андреев, Михаил*: История на българската буржоазна държава и право 1878–1917, p. 197.

74 Закон за устройството на съдилищата, Държавен вестник, issue 7, 12 (24) January 1899.

the number of law students reached 94. At the beginning, the degree course lasted for three years, but it was soon lengthened to four years.[75] Prior to the establishment of Sofia University's Faculty of Law, all professional Bulgarian jurists had been forced to receive their higher legal education abroad. Since this was an expensive endeavor, it is unsurprising that few people in Bulgaria had a law degree prior to the establishment of domestic higher legal education. Research into the Bulgarian intelligentsia in the late Ottoman period concluded that in 1878 there were only 51 Bulgarians with a law degree.[76] The scarcity of people with a higher education in law afforded those that had enjoyed such an education a wide range of career paths, many of which, such as politics, diplomacy and business, were better paid and/or were considered more prestigious that the judgeship. Moreover, many people with higher legal education chose to be lawyers rather than judges or prosecutors for the better income and greater freedom it gave them.[77] The problem was especially acute in smaller provincial courts, compared with the Supreme Court in Sofia, which was staffed by highly trained jurists who had received their higher legal education abroad, usually in Germany and Russia. Many Supreme Court judges, like P. Danchov, V. Marinov, G. Zgurev and A. Kableshkov, were also among the first professors at Sofia University's Faculty of Law.[78]

3.1.3.3 Enforcement of judicial decisions

The 1880 Law on the Organization of the Courts did not regulate the enforcement of the decisions of the justices of the peace. Enforcement continued to be organized according to the 1878 Provisional Rules on the Organization of the Judiciary in Bulgaria: the justice of peace issued a writ of execution, which was executed by the police and municipal authorities. The 1880 Law on the Organization of the Courts did, however, regulate the execution of the decisions of the district courts; it

75 *Паев, Костадин*: Историята на българската държава и право и юридическото образование, Управление и образование, vol. 5 (2009), no. 3, pp. 202–214.

76 *Аврамова, Румяна/Василева, Весела/Генчев, Николай/Давчева, Даниела/Даскалова, Красимира/Димитрова, Дочка/Еленкова, Ваня/Куюмджиева, Миглена*: Българска възрожденска интелигенция: Учители, свещеници, монаси, висши духовници, аптекари, писатели, издатели, книжари, търговци, военни... : Енциклопедия, Sofia 1988, pp. 91, 317, pp. 665–666.

77 For example, Konstantiv Stoilov, the prime minister, whose government left the most profound trace in the Bulgarian legal and judicial system in the pre-WWI period, studied civil law in Paris and had a PhD in Legal Studies from the University of Heidelberg. Instead of going into the judicial system, Stoilov chose politics and diplomacy as his profession. His government (1894–1899) passed a series of key legal acts, such as the Penal Law (1896), the Commercial Law (1898) and the Law on the Organization of the Courts (1899). His career is indicative for the professional choices of people with higher education in the newly liberated Bulgarian state, who formed a large part of the political and business elite of the country.

78 *Андреев, Михаил*: История на българската буржоазна държава и право 1878–1917, pp. 224–232.

stipulated the appointment of bailiffs for each district court whose function was to enforce its decisions (in case of non-compliance they were assisted by the police).[79] In 1897, alongside the new Commercial Law, the Law on Injunctive Proceedings was also passed. It tried to address complaints of slow enforcement procedures in cases of default payments. To ensure that the simplification of procedures would not proliferate frauds, the Law was only applicable to monetary claims supported by a notarized document, bills of exchange and promissory notes; claims between merchants; and claims for vacating rented premises.[80]

3.2 Reforms in the legal system (1877–1890s)

3.2.1 The 1893 Law on Obligations and Contracts

In 1878, when Bulgaria seceded from the Ottoman Empire, the antecedent Ottoman legislation continued to be the law of the land in the Bulgarian Principality. Thus, the Ottoman civil code *(Mecelle)* continued to be the main source of civil law in the new state for the first years of its existence. However, the fact that its provisions were based on the principles of Islamic law was often viewed by contemporary Bulgarian jurists as a weakness and a drawback. The new state's drive towards modernization was generally interpreted as a process of westernization and de-Ottomanization, so the Bulgarian legislature viewed the continued application of Ottoman laws as inconsistent with the economic needs and modernizing aspirations of the new state. Together with the *Mecelle*'s perceived incompleteness (i.e. its lack of general provisions concerning the general principles of contract law and its lack of provisions on statute of limitations etc.), this was among the key arguments in favor of reform, as compiled by the Minister of Justice in a report concerning contract law in the Principality.[81]

Thus, the Law on Obligations and Contracts was passed on 5 (17) December 1892 and came into force on 1 (12) March 1893. The Law was indirectly based on the French *Code civil*, insofar as it primarily took the form of the Italian civil code of 1865 (with some provisions additionally borrowed from the Spanish civil code). The first part of the Law on Obligations and Contracts regulated the general principles of contract law, such as the definition of a contract and its characteristics, i.e. who could be a contractual party and their attendant legal statuses; the effects of a contract; its creation and interpretation; and its termination. The second part of the Law regulated the following types of contracts: (1) sale; (2) barter; (3) lease,

---

79 *Джамбазов, Ангел*: op. cit., pp. 52, 58–59, 66–67.

80 Закон за заповедното съдопроизводство, Държавен вестник, issue 277, 15 (27) December 1897.

81 *Андреев, Михаил*: История на българската буржоазна държава и право 1878–1917, p. 119.

covering effects, labor, livestock and the *métayage*; (4) partnership, both general and particular; (5) power of attorney; (6) conciliatory agreement; (7) annuity; (8) insurance; (9) aleatory contracts, most notably betting; (10) loan, including consumption loans; (11) deposit and sequester; (12) security; and (13) pledge. Of these, the sale contract was regulated in the most detail, due to its widespread use in everyday life and trade.

Since the Bulgarian state had not adopted a comprehensive civil code and due to the fact that the 1850 CL did not contain any detailed regulations on commercial transactions, the 1893 Law on Obligations and Contracts effectively regulated commercial transactions as well. As both the 1850 and 1893 Laws were based on the French Napoleonic codes, they complemented each other coherently, without many problems. The brief period between the coming into force of the 1893 Law on Obligations and Contracts and 1898 Commercial Law was the period of the greatest coherence in nineteenth century Bulgarian commercial law history, since the system was governed according to the principles of only a single legal tradition, that being the French.

3.2.2 The 1898 Commercial Law

Initially, the 1850 CL had been regarded as compatible with the newly independent Bulgaria's drive towards modernization and westernization, since it was borrowed from the French legal tradition. However, it was not based on contemporary French legislation but rather on the 1807 Napoleonic code, which included some even older provisions dating back to the seventeenth century *Code Savary*. From the early 1890s onward, the 1850 CL came increasingly under attack for its outdated provisions reflecting realities long outlived. It was also criticized for the incompleteness of its provisions, particularly those regulating companies, bills of exchange and bankruptcy.[82]

In 1891, for example, a group of Kiustendil merchants addressed the Parliament with concerns over the 1850 CL's bankruptcy procedures. According to them, the current legislation was too lax, allowing unscrupulous businessmen to commit fraud and accumulate unlawful gains. The Foreign Ministry (then in the process of concluding Bulgaria's first trade agreements) also addressed the Ministry of Justice expressing its concerns about the slow bankruptcy procedures and officially requested a new commercial code reflecting contemporary European legal development and innovations. Following this request, in 1895 the Ministry of Justice appointed a special commission consisting of Ministry of Justice officials, members of the Supreme Court of Cassation and public prosecutors, which was tasked with

82 *Токушев, Димитър*: op. cit., p. 203.

preparing a new commercial code. Unfortunately, the commission did not leave any written records identifying their reasons for preferring different European legal traditions for different parts of their bill. The ensuing draft law was primarily based on the German and French legal traditions, albeit indirectly. The parts of the law regulating the general principals of commercial law and those concerning commercial contracts, transactions, companies and financial instruments (e.g. bills of exchange, promissory notes, checks) were borrowed largely from the 1875 Hungarian Commercial Law and the 1876 Hungarian Law on the Bills of Exchange, which were themselves based on German legal norms. By contrast, bankruptcy was modelled on the provisions of the 1887 Romanian Commercial Law, which was based on the 1883 Italian Commercial Code, which was, in turn, heavily influenced by the French legal tradition. The bill was passed through the Parliament with almost no changes in February 1897, was promulgated in May 1897 and came into force on 1 (12) January 1898.[83]

The contents of the first book of the 1898 CL largely reproduced the 1875 Hungarian Commercial Law with the exception of Arts. 4–13 of Chapter One "On Merchants" and Chapter Four "On Commercial Books" of Section One, Part One as well as Chapter 12 "On Checks" of Section Three, Part One which were borrowed from Romanian Commercial Law.[84] The second book, which concerned bankruptcy, was also based on Romanian law. Hence, with the 1898 Commercial Law the Bulgarian legislature took the rather unorthodox decision to regulate commercial activities in Bulgaria under the norms of two different legal traditions. Moreover, as critics of the law were quick to point out, the vast majority of the provisions had been simply translated, without any attempts having been made by the legislature to unite them into a consistent and coherent legal framework. Not only was the 1898 Commercial Law a compilation of legal provisions belonging to two different legal families, but it was also not always consistent with the civil law, e.g. with the 1893 Law on Contracts and Obligations, to which it referred and to which it also granted subsidiary application in commercial disputes.[85] This hybrid approach meant that the same transaction could foreseeably be subject to different legal regimes, depending on the legal status of the contractors. A transaction was treated as commercial and regulated by the 1898 CL if concluded by a merchant as part of his profession, but was otherwise regulated by the 1893 Law on Contracts and Obligations.

The 1898 Commercial Law consisted of 833 articles, organized into two books and 33 chapters. Its content included general rules, a first section on merchants,

83 *Ганев, Венелин*: Историческо развитие на несъстоятелността в главните негови моменти; *Ганев, Венелин*: Истор-ическо развитие на търговското право, pp. 33–38.

84 *Токушев, Димитър*: op. cit., p. 205.

85 *Андреев, Михаил*: История на българската буржоазна държава и право 1878–1917, pp. 133–134.

types of companies, and commercial transactions, a second section on bankruptcy, and final provisions.

3.2.2.1 Company law

The first book of the 1898 Commercial Law was dedicated to the regulation of mercantile activities. Pursuant to Art. 2, a merchant was legally defined as a person engaging in commercial transactions in a professional capacity under their own names. A merchant could be either a natural or a legal person, the latter defined as a "commercial company" and accordingly regulated in Books 2–5 (Arts. 68–271) of the Commercial Law. The regime for acquiring the status of a merchant was quite liberal and open to all natural persons, although minors and married women required permission to do so by their parents, guardians or husbands.

Like the 1850 CL, the 1898 CL required each merchant to keep three types of ledgers: a journal containing daily descriptions of all transactions; an inventory and balance book of all their property, including personal funds; and a copybook for their commercial correspondence. The journal and the inventory and balance book were to be presented at the end of each year for notarization.[86]

Arts. 45–59 of the Commercial Law regulated the rights of company managers to represent their companies. Their rights to sign documents on behalf of the company were almost unlimited, the only exception being their inability to sell or mortgage real estate without a special power of attorney from the owner(s). Companies could also appoint commercial agents with limited rights of representation before third parties, in their role as company officials.[87]

The 1898 Commercial Law recognized four types of business associations: (1) general partnerships, (2) limited partnerships (simple or with shares), (3) joint-stock companies and (4) cooperatives. The 1898 Commercial Law did not introduce any major legal innovations with regard to general and limited partnerships as compared to the 1850 CL, but rather regulated some aspects thereof in more detail. For example, the 1898 CL contained provisions on what rights and responsibilities between partners were presumed in absence of a contract. The 1898 Law also ensured greater transparency and accountability through the introduction of commercial registers, administered by the local court, and making part of the companies' information public through publications in the press. The Law also included a five-year statute of limitations for creditors' claims, as well as regulation to what extent limited partners could represent the company without proper

86 Търговски закон, Sofia 1897, pp. 10–13 (Arts. 31–44).

87 Ibid., pp. 13–17 (Arts. 45–59).

authorization (i.e. without managerial contract or power of attorney) and without being treated as unlimited partners.[88]

The third type of business association regulated by the 1898 Commercial Law was the joint-stock company. Of all the types of business associations, joint-stock companies were the ones regulated most comprehensively, since their structure and organization were by far the most sophisticated, but also because they were perceived to present the greatest risk in terms of fraud. The establishment process of joint-stock companies in comparison to the 1850 CL was more liberal as it did not require special permission. According to Art. 152, joint-stock companies were considered lawfully founded if a set of linked criteria had been satisfied: (1) a notarized subscription existed, which confirmed that its capital had been raised; (2) 30% of this capital had been deposited; and (3) the company's statute had been drawn up and deposited in the commercial register of its headquarters' local district court. The most important information regarding relations with third parties were to be made public. The 1898 CL further required that, within the two months following the period in which the subscription was to be confirmed, a founding assembly for the company had to be convened. After ensuring that all capital-related requirements were met, the assembly could establish the new company, approve its statutes, and elect its first management and supervisory boards. The Law stipulated a list of requirements a joint-stock company statute should regulate; these included:

- the basic characteristics of the company, i.e. its name, headquarters, activities etc.;
- the management of capital, i.e. the type of shares the company would issue and the rights of its shareholders;
- its management and supervisory bodies; and
- its accountability and transparency policy.

A joint-stock company's shares could either be 'registered' or 'upon presentation'. The former carried the name of the shareholder and had to be entered into the company's registers in order to be valid. The latter were more easily tradable, as it was only necessary to present the shares upon request (i.e. when receiving dividends or voting in the company's general meeting).[89]

Limited liability, joint-stock companies' most important feature, remained the same in both the 1850 and 1898 Commercial Laws. Shareholders continued to be liable only to the extent of their share in the company's capital and the company's management and supervisory bodies faced personal financial sanctions only in cases of fraud, falsification and other unlawful actions. However, the 1898 Law was

---

88 Ibid., pp. 20–43 (Arts. 68–147).

89 Ibid., pp. 43–73 (Arts. 148–238).

much more detailed in its regulations, including penal sanctions for management officials and representatives.

The last type of business entity regulated by the 1898 Law were cooperative associations. Although such organizations did exist both in the Ottoman Empire and in the Principality of Bulgaria (e.g. in the form of mutual agricultural funds), they were not object to specific regulation. The 1898 CL did regulate such entities, whose purpose was to give impetus to banking, industry or agriculture through mutuality or cooperation. They included the following types of cooperatives: (1) credit associations, (2) associations for joint production and other related activities, (3) consumer associations, (4) associations for the construction of residential buildings and (5) mutual insurance associations.[90] These articles were repealed in 1907 due to the enactment of the Law on Cooperative Associations the same year.

Although German law had already introduced the concept of a limited liability company *(Gesellschaft mit beschränkter Haftung – GmbH)* in 1892, the Bulgarian legislature did not include this form of enterprise in the 1898 Commercial Law. Fears that limited liability would be used fraudulently delayed the adoption of this type of business company in Bulgaria until after the First World War in 1924.

3.2.2.2 *Transactions*

The third section of the 1898 CL's first part concerned commercial transactions. The type of transactions which were deemed commercial were fully enumerated, such transactions being divided into three categories by the Law: transactions that were always commercial, transactions which were commercial when undertaken professionally and transactions done by a merchant in support of his trade (Arts. 279, 280 and 281). Since the transactions in the last two categories were considered commercial only if concluded by a merchant, it was the first category, that of the essentially commercial transactions, which were used to define the legal capacities of the merchant and, consequently, the scope of application of the 1898 Law. The essentially commercial transactions included: (1) the purchase or acquisition of goods or property for resale; (2) the delivery of the aforementioned goods or property; (3) the purchase or acquisition of securities or shares; (4) insurance; (5) the carriage of passengers or goods by sea and the conclusion of maritime loans with collateral; and (6) bills of exchanges and promissory notes. The Law provided general principles of commercial transactions followed by more detailed provisions covering the most common type of commercial transactions and contracts, such as sale, commission, freight forwarding, transport, use of public warehouses, publication, agency, insurance, use of bills of exchange, promissory notes, and checks.[91]

90 Ibid., pp. 73–84 (Arts. 239–271).

91 Ibid., pp. 87–192 (Arts. 279–648).

3.2.2.3 Bankruptcy

The second part of the 1898 Law (Arts. 649–822) was dedicated to bankruptcy procedures. This was considered a matter of major importance, since the incompleteness of the 1850 Commercial Law was blamed for failing to prevent the proliferation of fraudulent bankruptcy schemes. Under the new Law, any merchant who had ceased paying their maturing liabilities was considered insolvent. Bankruptcy was declared by court order at the request of the insolvent trader(s), at the request of one or more of their creditors, or ex officio by the court. Under the insolvency order, the court would appoint one of its members as a clerk responsible for managing the insolvency procedure. The clerk also acted as a temporary liquidator, until the creditors appointed a permanent liquidator. In addition, the property of the trader was sealed, and a deadline was set for the creditors to file their claims. Criminal proceedings against the trader were initiated alongside the insolvency proceedings under the Chapter on "Bankruptcy and Damage to Creditors" of the Criminal Code. The two proceedings were independent of one another. As with the 1850 CL, the debtor and creditors were given the opportunity to conclude an agreement for deferred payment called a *concordato*, which needed court approval. If such an agreement was not achieved, following a lengthy procedure, the property of the insolvent trader would be auctioned, the resulting sum of which would be used to satisfy the claims of the creditors. While not introducing any major changes in the bankruptcy regulations, the 1898 Law ensured that the transactions of insolvent merchants could be better scrutinized and provided greater protection for creditors.[92]

The 1898 Law did not cover maritime trade, which was instead regulated in Bulgaria by the Ottoman Law on Maritime Commerce until 1908.

4. Conclusion

Bulgaria's first encounters with Western commercial law occurred when it was still under Ottoman rule. In 1840 the first specialized commercial court in the Ottoman Empire was created in Istanbul. Foreigners and foreign protégés, as well as Ottoman *beratlı* merchants, were given access to this new institution and the right to transfer their cases from a provincial court to the capital. In 1847 the first provincial commercial courts were established in the major Balkan towns of Edirne and Salonica and by the early 1850s such commercial courts had started to appear in Ottoman Bulgaria as well. Until the adoption of the 1860 Supplement to the Commercial Law the structure and organization of these new commercial courts

92 Ibid., pp. 192–256 (Arts. 649–822).

mirrored that of the Istanbul Commercial Court, with access similarly restricted to privileged classes of merchants. In the 1840s and 1850s, the existence of privileged groups of merchants with preferential access to judicial institutions during this period created a pluralistic legal system which afforded those privileged classes opportunities for 'forum shopping'.

In 1850, a new Commercial Law was adopted which displaced the antecedent Islamic commercial law and made substantial changes to the framework which it had established. Most notably, the 1850 CL changed company law, commercial documentation standards, debt and interest regulation, bankruptcy proceeding and introduced new forms of legal incorporation, such as the joint-stock company. Joint-stock companies allowed the accumulation of large sums of capital in a relatively short time and thus facilitated the financing of larger business ventures. With regard to bankruptcy, the 1850 CL provided greater protection for creditors against fraud and malicious bankruptcies, while also permitting agreements to be made between insolvent merchants and their creditors through the *concordato* instrument. The detailed regulation of bills of exchange and promissory notes as payment instruments established better mechanisms through which merchants could be protected against unfulfilled financial obligations, such as through the regulation of interest on default payments. Unlike Shari'a, which made extensive use of oral testimony (as well as of written documents), the new commercial laws privileged written over oral evidence. Furthermore, the new regulations reduced the possibility of fraud through the use of bribed witnesses and eliminated the discriminatory treatment of non-Muslim testimony.

In the early 1860s a new series of commercial law reforms ensured: the most important of these were the 1860 Supplement of the Commercial Law, 1861 Commercial Procedure Law and the 1863 Law on Maritime Commerce. The most significant change which occurred under the 1860 SCL was the opening of the commercial courts to all members of the merchant classes, regardless of whether they were members of the privileged class or not. The 1860 Law also reformed the internal organization and structure of the courts, which now included both government-appointed salaried officials and unpaid members elected by the local business communities. The adoption of the 1861 CPL codified procedure rules in commercial courts; it regulated in detail every step of the proceedings, creating a highly formalized judicial system as a result (especially in comparison to the relatively informal and flexible procedure rules in the *kadi* courts). Data from the Ottoman yearbooks reveal that the network of commercial courts was constantly expanding throughout the 1860s and 1870s. By the beginning of the Russo-Ottoman War in 1877 there was a dense network of sixteen commercial courts functioning in the territory of present-day Bulgaria. Quantitative data on commercial courts confirm that by the late 1860s/early 1870s commercial courts in Bulgaria were fully operational institutions and were dealing with significant workloads. They were primarily adjudicating cases between Ottoman citizens, rather than foreigners.

The secession of the Principality of Bulgaria did not immediately lead to major commercial law reform: the 1850 CL continued to be in force in the new Bulgarian state until the late 1890s when a new commercial code was passed. The 1898 Commercial Law introduced a series of innovative legal concepts to Bulgarian commercial law, such as new legal forms for business entities, new types of commercial transactions and new kinds of financial instruments. With regard to existing types of business association, such as partnerships (limited and unlimited) and joint-stock companies, the 1898 Law sought to fill the lacunae and solve the problems of the old regime by, for example, improving transparency for such companies with the creation of commercial registers and publication requirements for certain types of information. Additionally, the Law reformed and updated bankruptcy procedures to address concerns and complaints about insufficient protection from fraudulent bankruptcies.

A reorganization of the judicial system followed immediately after the establishment of the new Bulgarian state. The 1880 Law on the Organization of the Courts abolished the separate commercial courts and equalized judicial treatment of commercial and other civil law cases. The 1899 Law on the Organization of the Courts, while not making significant changes to the structure of the judicial system, introduced new regulations concerning judicial personnel aimed at improving their professional qualifications, as well as their independence.

In the history of Bulgarian commercial law of the period spanning the final decades of Ottoman rule and the first decades of the newly established Principality, there was a significant degree of continuity. This is especially true with regard to statutory commercial law; the 1850 Commercial Law remaining the established commercial law of the land for almost half a century, outlasting political upheavals, wars and changes in sovereignty. The judicial system, meanwhile, was subject to more frequent reforms, with significant reforms affecting it almost every twenty years (in 1840, 1860, 1880 and 1899).

Zoran S. Mirković

The Beginnings of Commercial Law in Serbia 1840–1860

1. Introduction

1.1 Serbian Merchants and Freedom of Trade in the Territory of the Ottoman Empire from 1830 onwards

By virtue of the 1830 Sultan's Hatt-i Sharif, the former Belgrade Pashalik was granted autonomous status and became the Principality of Serbia. The fifth item of the Hatt-i Sharif gave Serbian merchants the right to trade throughout the Ottoman Empire. They had to possess a passport, issued by the Serbian Prince with the approval of the Sublime Porte. Serbian merchants were able to move and trade freely throughout the Empire without harassment or financial burdens.[1] The Sultan's firmans of 1837 and 1839 on the rights of Serbian merchants in the Ottoman Empire and in the vassal principalities of that Empire – Wallachia and Moldavia respectively – testify to the sizeable number and importance of colonies of Serbian merchants. The 1837 Sultan's firman issued to the qadi of Constantinople mentions Serbian merchants who traded with Europe. These merchants were granted a free trade decree. They were entitled to elect their two representatives for a period of one year to adjudicate in commercial matters among them. At the request of Prince Miloš, the Sultan ordered that no one was to interfere in trade affairs of Serbs who had free trade decrees, except for Serbia's envoy to Constantinople. He had the authority to punish Serbian merchants, through an Ottoman official.

Sultan Abdulmejid, who acceded to the throne in 1839, confirmed the firman on the right of an official appointed to Wallachia and Moldavia by the Serbian Prince to administer justice among Serbian merchants there. He issued an order to that effect to the princes of Wallachia and Moldavia.[2]

---

1 *Matić, Dimitrije*: Javno pravo Knjažestva Srbije, Beograd 1851, pp. 36–37.

2 Ibid., pp. 94–98.

1.2 The so-called Turkish Constitution and Internal Free Trade

Prince Miloš Obrenović, the leader of the Second Serbian Uprising in 1815, was the Prince of the Principality of Serbia until June 1839.[3] Under his rule, internal trade was not free. Trade could only be conducted with the permission of the authorities. Miloš allegedly wanted to save farmers from unscrupulous merchants. Therefore, only certain persons were allowed to engage in trade and even then, only on specific terms. Serbian farmers had land, but they did not have capital or an opportunity to get a loan. Trade was the only way for them to get the money needed to pay taxes and to buy the things they needed, which they did not produce by themselves. That is why farmers under Miloš were requesting freedom of trade. They were asking for freedom to trade in their agricultural produce and raw materials, primarily live cattle. Live cattle were the main export item of the then Serbia, while all other agricultural products were "of secondary importance".[4]

The so-called Turkish Constitution of December 1838 proclaimed the principle of freedom of trade (Article 45). That constitution was read in Belgrade in February 1839. With freedom of trade, the Constitution met a great popular need. Freedom of trade was also one of the main items of the constitution-defenders' program. After the adoption of the Constitution, that political group forced Prince Miloš to abdicate and took over power.

After the fall of Prince Miloš, trade was free. Farmers were given the opportunity to trade in their agricultural products, predominantly cattle. Instead of selling cattle to a merchant designated by the government, at the price fixed by that government, the farmer could instead sell them to whomever offered a good price. Freedom of trade meant freedom to sell and buy agricultural products.

By giving farmers freedom to trade, the government left trade almost unregulated. Admittedly, the Guild Decree was passed in 1847 but it only dealt with the internal organization of the merchants' profession. Freedom of trade was understood not only as the absence of restrictions, but also regulations. Only the regulations laid

---

3 In the territory of the Belgrade Pashalik, in 1804 Serbs rose in rebellion against the Dahis (renegades from the Ottoman Empire) who had usurped power from the legal Ottoman authorities. That is when the event known as the First Serbian Uprising began, which in the meantime turned into a revolt against the Ottoman rule in general. That uprising was quelled in the autumn of 1813. After the repression by the re-established Ottoman authorities, in the spring of 1815, Miloš Obrenović staged a rebellion known as the Second Serbian Uprising. In early November 1815, an unwritten agreement was reached between the leader of the insurgents, Miloš Obrenović, and the Ottoman vizier, Marashli Ali Pasha. That agreement was confirmed the following year, 1816, by the sultan's decrees *(bérats)*. Finally, in 1830, the Sultan issued the *Hatt-i Sharif*, by virtue of which the Belgrade Pashalik became the Principality of Serbia and was granted autonomous status within the Ottoman Empire.

4 *Jovanović, Slobodan*: Ustavobranitelji i njihova vlada. Druga vlada Miloša i Mihaila, Sabrana dela, vol. 3, Beograd 1990, p. 88.

down by the general 1844 Civil Code were applied.[5] The Principality of Serbia's trade relations were governed by agreements between the Ottoman and the Austrian Empires, which provided for low tariffs of 3% based on the goods' value, with incidental fees at a rate of 2%.[6]

1.3 System of Capitulations

For the first time in 1535, the Ottoman Empire accepted by capitulation "the competence of the French consulate in all kinds of legal proceedings relating to merchants, citizens of this country."[7] The system of capitulations, which was in place between the Ottoman Empire and other states, was applicable to the citizens of those states, even after the establishment of the Serbian autonomous government in 1830.[8] This meant that many foreigners, who conducted business in the Principality of Serbia, predominantly in Belgrade, were exempted from the Serbian legal order. These foreigners, most of whom were from the Austrian Empire, then from Prussia[9], were engaged in trading and running artisan shops and taverns. Although numerous, they were not under the jurisdiction of the Serbian administrative and judicial authorities, unless permitted to be by their consulates. The number of those covered by this advantageous system was not negligible, which is evidenced by the fact that aliens (foreign subjects) accounted for about 7% of the population of the city of Belgrade in 1846.[10]

The system of capitulations remained an obstacle to the establishment of jurisdiction and the full implementation of laws therein, within the Principality of Serbia, for a long time. Moreover, the great powers did not waive their right to exercise

---

5 Ibid., pp. 88–92; "The constitution had established virtual free trade, internal and external. The value of livestock exports to the Habsburg dominions continued to rise, and the value of imports likewise, creating a small trade surplus. The merchant class, who had moved upwards from the peasantry, was turning to a European lifestyle by the 1850s; low Ottoman tariffs, still applicable to Serbia, encouraged the influx of foreign goods ... trade profits went into imports" (*Pavlović, Stevan K.*: Srbija-istorija iza imena, Prevela sa engleskog Ivana Gazikalović-Pavlović, Beograd 2004, p. 56 (English edition of this book: *Pavlowitch, Stevan K.*: Serbia: The History Behind the Name, London 2002)).

6 *Jovanović, Slobodan*: op. cit. p. 93.

7 This situation lasted until the Lausanne Peace Treaty between the Republic of Turkey and the Western countries (of 25 July 1923), which abolished the system of capitulations, i.e., courts before the consulates of foreign states (as well as the jurisdiction of non-Muslim communities), *Ihsanoğlu, Ekmeleddin* (ed.): Historija osmanske države i civilizacije, Istanbul and Sarajevo 2004, pp. 581–582.

8 For more information on consulates and capitulations in the Ottoman Empire see *Hattenhauer, Hans*: Europäische Rechtsgeschichte, 4. Auflage, Heidelberg 2004, pp. 533–538.

9 This data was provided by a high police official and the administrator of the City of Belgrade, *Hristić, Nikola*: Memoari 1840–1842, Beograd 2006, p. 180.

10 *Čubrilović, Vasa* (ed.): Istorija Beograda-devetnaesti vek, 2, Beograd 1974, p. 526.

consular jurisdiction over their citizens in Serbia, granted to them under the previously concluded treaties with the Ottoman Empire. Even in the Treaty of Berlin dated 13 July 1878, by which they recognized the independence of the Principality of Serbia. Article 37 stipulated: "The immunities and privileges of foreign subjects, as well as the rights of Consular jurisdiction and protection, as at present existing, shall remain in full force so long as they shall not have been modified by mutual consent between the Principality and the Powers concerned. "[11]

2. Court of the City of Belgrade

2.1 Establishment

The establishment of the Court of the City of Belgrade was a result of the progress made in trade and the related rise in trade disputes, as well as the system of capitulations, though indirectly.

On 23 June 1841, the Ministry of Justice put forward a proposal to establish this court to adjudicate disputes between the residents of Belgrade and both foreigners and the other residents of the then Serbia. The underlying reason for this proposal was the increase in the number of trade disputes. The first instance court, the Belgrade District Court, could not deal with these trade disputes on top of its regular jurisdiction. It was also proposed that the Court of the City of Belgrade would have a president, three members and a court secretary, who would be lawyers by education with experience in practicing law. The Ministry of Justice was convinced that such a court, composed of trained lawyers, would eliminate the frequent objections of foreign consuls to Serbian courts and consolidate the confidence in the new court.[12]

On 4 July 1841, the Council approved the establishment of the Court of the City of Belgrade, with the proviso that the president, members of the Court and the court secretary be elected from among the ranks of "local capable officials". The Ministry, unlike the Council, intended to fill the vacancies for court staff through a competitive process. This implied selecting the most professionally capable and the most morally upright candidates, be they locals or outsiders, primarily from the Habsburg Empire. The Council was of a different opinion however, as expressed in its reply dated 22 September 1841. The Council considered that the new court needed both: those who had completed studies of legal sciences and those who acquired the necessary knowledge in practice. The Council underscored that it was necessary for the people to have confidence in their courts and that the question

11 *Vojdović, Mihailo* (ed.): Srbija 1878, Dokumenti, Beograd 1978, pp. 565–571.

12 *Jovanović, Aleksa*: Postanak prvostepenog suda varoši Beograda, Beograd 1904, p. 5.

of who they would trust more, those they already knew or foreigners, was a very serious question. The Council recalled that, in a dispute before the court, one party had to lose and, if a native lost the dispute, he would always put the blame on the judge he did not know, rather than on the law failing to support his claim. He would say that the foreign judge had sided with his man, a foreigner.

Finally, on 10 October 1841, Serbia's Prince Mihailo Obrenović signed a decree on the establishment of the Court of the City of Belgrade. It was a special court that was supposed to adjudicate trade disputes between residents of Belgrade and foreigners, on the one hand, and residents from other parts of Serbia, on the other. It belonged to the category of district courts. The reason cited for the establishment of the Court of the City of Belgrade was the fact that the Belgrade District Court could not "cope with" with trade disputes, whose number was increasing on a daily basis.[13]

In the course of February 1842, the court was provided with a building, which had previously housed the Ministry of the Interior. The President and two members of the Court of the City of Belgrade took an oath on 12 March 1842, and four days later they started working. On that day, 16 March, the Ministry of Foreign Affairs sent the following documents to the Court for trials in disputes with foreigners:

- an excerpt from the book *Guide Diplomatique*, on the privileges of foreign consuls in the Ottoman Empire,
- a copy of the Požarevac Trade Agreement, which concerned relations between the Habsburg and Ottoman Empires, especially the fifth item on the proceedings before the Ottoman courts, and
- an article on the freedoms enjoyed by Austrian merchants in the Ottoman Empire.

Moreover, the Ministry of Foreign Affairs promised the court direct assistance, if and when disputes arose in which the consuls would invoke the mentioned or other international agreements. On the same day, 16 March 1842, the Ministry of Foreign Affairs informed foreign consuls that the Court of the City of Belgrade had commenced its work and they were asked to inform their citizens to approach the court in disputes when they sued or were sued. Despite some attempts from the Austrian and Ottoman sides to call the court's jurisdiction into question, the Court of the City of Belgrade took over the trials of the disputes entrusted to it.[14]

Nevertheless, the Circular of 14 November 1853 shows that there were problems and that things were not developing as planned. It reiterated that the Court of the

13 *Петровићь, Ђорђе* (ed.): Ръчникь закона, уредба и уредбены прописа и пр. и пр. изданы у Княжеству Србіи одь 1827. до половине 1854. год., Beograd 1856, p. 467 (hereinafter: Ръчникь закона, уредба и уредбены прописа).

14 *Jovanović, Aleksa*: op. cit., pp. 23–24.

City of Belgrade was the competent court for all foreigners who lived in Serbia in their disputes with Serbian residents. The courts were ordered to refer the parties to these disputes directly to the Court of the City of Belgrade. That court would receive the complaint, conduct the investigation, hold the hearing and hand down the judgment.[15]

2.2 Judges and Court Staff

Both the recollections of contemporaries and the official data confirm the lack of professional qualifications on the part of the Serbian judges of that time.[16]

The appointment of the best staff to the Court of the City of Belgrade was the result of the awareness of its significance and of the desire for it to gain trust as it was supposed to try foreigners as well. By virtue of the decree of 10 December 1841, the staff appointed to the newly established court included Jakov Dimšić as court secretary, Stefan Dimitrijević as court clerk and Teodor Grujović and Spiridon Radosavljević as civil-service trainees. Based on the available evidence, we can conclude that they were qualified for these jobs. Dimšić[17] had a degree in "philosophy and Hungarian law".[18] Dimitrijević was a lawyer in "German and Hungarian law". Grujović completed his law degree with distinction at the Belgrade Lyceum. The scarce data on Radosavljević shows that he was a diligent court trainee.

After that, by virtue of a decree of 29 December 1841, the following staff members were appointed: Sava Šilić, former Department Head at the Ministry of Justice, as the Court President; Venijamin Rozmirović, Secretary General of the Council, as the first member of the Court; and Andrija Koviljac, Secretary of the Court of

---

15 Рѣчникъ закона, уредба и уредбены прописа, p. 467.

16 In their recollections of the courts in the 1840s and beyond, this is confirmed by Đorđe Cenić, professor, minister, prime minister (*Cenić, Đorđe*: Je li prekoračena suma određena budžetom na penzioniranje činovnika za 1874. god.?, Beograd 1876, p. 24) and Nikola Hristić, judge, president of the court, minister, prime minister (*Hristić, Nikola*: Memoari 1840–1842, pp. 113–114).

17 Jakov Dimšić was court secretary from 10 December 1841 to 17 February 1842, when he returned to the position of secretary of the Court of Appeals, which is the duty he had performed as of 17 February 1839 (Archives of Serbia, State Council – Belgrade, roll 132, sh. 219–220 (Arhiv Srbije, Državni savet – Beograd; hereinafter: AS, DS)).

18 References to philosophy and law or "Hungarian law" point to the royal academies of law in the Hungarian lands of the Habsburg Monarchy, where the first two years were devoted to the studies of philosophy, and the other two (or three) years to the studies of law. See *Mirković, Zoran S.*: Pravne studije krajem XVIII i početkom XIX veka i beogradska Velika škola 1808–1813. godine, Anali Pravnog fakulteta u Beogradu, vol. 56 (2008), no. 1, pp. 126–149; *Mirkovic, Zoran S.*: Die Anfänge des Rechtsstudium im Serbien der Neuzeit und die Juristenausbildung in der Habsburgermonarchie (ein Beispiel des Rechtstransfers), The Annals of the Faculty of Law in Belgrade – Belgrade Law Review, vol. 58 (2010), no. 3, pp. 151–162.

Appeals, as the second member.[19] The President of the Court, Šilić, "completed his studies in Hungary and passed the exam at the Hungarian Supreme Court, following a regular path, and became a lawyer in 1828."[20] Regarding Rozmirović, it can be said with near-certainty that he was a trained lawyer. He subsequently became a cassation court judge. Regarding Koviljac, it can be assumed that he was a lawyer by education.

However, three years later, the quality of the judicial part of the Court of the City of Belgrade deteriorated for some reason. The report of the Ministry of Justice to the Council for 1844 reveals that there were no lawyers among the judges of the district courts, the Court of the City of Belgrade and the Court of Appeals.[21] The situation was as follows: eighteen judges were illiterate, seven were barely literate ("can read and write a little"), forteen had completed primary ("normal") school and six had education beyond primary school (three had completed gymnasium, one had graduated from a seminary and two from some "military schools in Russia"). There is no data on the presidents of these courts. It is evident from the report that in a large number of courts the clerical part of the court compensated for the modest knowledge of the judges with their own qualifications. This is very apparent in the case of the Court of the City of Belgrade. In this Court, apart from the President of the Court, Venijamin Rozmirović, the situation with the three judges was as follows. Jovan Dimitrijević had completed primary ("normal") Serbian and German school in his place of birth, Irig, and had attended the gymnasium and the seminary in Sremski Karlovci. Teodor Petrović had completed primary school and certain "Greek and Turkish schools in Constantinople", while Stevan Aranicki had completed gymnasium. The clerical part of the court topped the judges by far in terms of their legal education. The Secretary of the Court from 21 October 1842, Jefrem Bozic, graduated from the gymnasium in Sremski Karlovci, as well as having studied philosophy and "Hungarian law" in Pozsony. Archivist Jovan Petrovic had attended Greek and Serbian primary school and gymnasium and had studied philosophy and Hungarian law in Pest, in addition to having passed the bar exam at the Royal Court in Pest. Grade I clerk Petar Radovanović graduated from the Kragujevac gymnasium, the philosophy department and from the legal department of the Lyceum in Belgrade. Grade II clerk Kosta Jačmenić graduated from the Kragujevac Gymnasium and earned a degree in philosophy and law from the Lyceum in Belgrade.[22]

Aware of such a situation in the courts, the Ministry of Justice issued a Circular Letter on 23 February 1843. The Circular Letter instructed "literate members of

---

19 *Jovanović, Aleksa*: op. cit., pp. 18–21.

20 AS, DS, roll 132, sh. 204–205.

21 AS, DS, roll 132, sh. 216–329.

22 AS, DS, roll 132, sh. 227–238.

the court, especially the court secretary and the junior staff" to make every effort to memorize, "perfectly understand" and apply all the regulations necessary for trials.[23] A reader of this Circular Letter has the impression that knowledge of the regulations was left to the clerical part of the court, while the judges, as illiterate dignitaries and authority figures, had to only administer justice in the usual way, without going into specifics of the regulations.

An uneducated judge, who is not a lawyer, rules in a society without written laws by basing their judgments on fairness, common sense and customary norms. An honest and wise man who knew people and circumstances and enjoyed the trust of the community could make a great judge. Staff comprising such people and a court clerk, who would meet the requirements related to literacy and the minimum knowledge of court proceedings and its forms, were perfectly suited to the tasks set before them in the period preceding the emergence of written laws.

3. Case Law on Trade Disputes

3.1 Statistics for 1844, 1845, 1858 and 1859

In the Historical Archives of Belgrade, which houses material relating to the Court of the City of Belgrade, the material on the period from the beginning of its work in 1842 to 1860 has not been preserved. Data on the work of that court is preserved in the annual reports of the Ministry of Justice and in several case files relating to the Court of Appeals.

The report of the Ministry of Justice for 1844 on civil litigation mentions the following disputes: patrimony, plot boundaries, land plots and buildings, watermills, inheritance, divisions, debts, rents and leases, partnerships, cancellation penalties, damages, damage to agricultural estates, compensations, lost cattle and guardianship. A total of 15 civil litigation categories were listed. There was no separate category for trade disputes. We can look for trade disputes in the following categories: debts, partnerships, cancellation penalties and compensations. They may, of course, also exist in the other identified categories.

The number of these disputes before the Court of the City of Belgrade in 1844 was as follows: debts – 428, partnerships – 3, cancellation penalties – 4, compensations – 99, out of 626 adjudicated civil disputes in total. Before all district courts, seventeen of them and the Court of the City of Belgrade, in 1844 the number of these disputes was as follows: debts – 2,056, partnerships – 38, cancellation penalties – 14, compensations – 633, out of 3,862 adjudicated civil disputes in total. The number

23 Рѣчникь закона, уредба и уредбены прописа, p. 432.

of these disputes before the Court of Appeals in 1844 was: debts – 127, partnerships – 3, cancellation penalties – 0, compensations – 60, out of 334 adjudicated civil disputes in total.[24]

Regarding civil litigation, the following can be derived from the report of the Ministry of Justice for 1845. In 1845, the Court of the City of Belgrade adjudicated 726 disputes for debts, 9 for partnerships, 15 for cancellation penalties, 19 for compensations, out of a total of 892 settled disputes. Overall, in 1845, in all 18 first-instance courts, 3,783 disputes were settled for debts, 57 for partnerships, 94 for cancellation penalties, 169 for compensations, out of a total of 6,299 settled disputes. In 1845, the Court of Appeals ruled on 230 disputes for debt, 9 for partnerships, 6 for cancellation penalties, 29 for compensations, out of a total of 681 settled disputes.[25] In 1858, before the Court of the City of Belgrade there were 2,030 disputes for debts, 18 for partnerships, 5 for cancellation penalties, 60 for compensation of damages, out of a total of 2,977 civil disputes. In all 18 first instance courts, there was a total of 31,530 disputes for debts, 139 for partnerships, 48 for cancellation penalties, 1,228 for compensation of damages, out of a total of 41,826 civil disputes.[26] In 1859, before the Court of the City of Belgrade there were 2,430 disputes for debts, 21 for partnerships, 131 for compensation of damages, out of 3,459 civil disputes in total. Before all 18 first instance courts, there were 33,489 disputes for debts, 177 for partnerships, 36 for cancellation penalties, 1,499 for compensation of damages, out of the total number of all civil disputes, which amounted to 46,778.[27]

3.2 Saved Trade Disputes

On 25 August 1842, an official document was written on behalf of the Principality of Serbia to the Court of the City of Belgrade regarding a lawsuit involving Georgji Spirt (although it is unclear who authored the letter, we can assume that it was the Ministry of Finance.) The plaintiff, Spirta, had a claim on the Principality of Serbia worth 505.65 thalers, for the alleged delivery of lead in 1822. The second claim was worth 339 thalers for the alleged trade of grain, which the plaintiff concluded with ex-prince Miloš in 1817. The official document referred to an invoice which showed that the 1822 debt for lead amounting to 505.65 thalers had been settled and that the receipt confirming its settlement had been signed by Spirta. However, the plaintiff stated in his complaint that he had been forced to sign that receipt, under duress, because Prince Miloš had threatened him with death if he did not sign. That document dismissed this claim and referred to a document signed by

24 AS, DS, roll 132, sh. 28.
25 AS, DS, roll 132, sh. 181.
26 AS, DS, roll 269, sh. 35–36.
27 AS, DS, roll 297, sh. 13–14.

the plaintiff himself to the effect that the debt was settled. The document then posed the following questions: Why did the plaintiff, as an Austrian citizen, fail to complain to the authorities of that state if he had suffered damage? Why did he not seek satisfaction from Prince Miloš in the period from 1822 to 1839, while he had been in power, by legal means and through the Austrian authorities? The plaintiff proposed one witness only. In the end, the document asked what would happen to trade transactions if someone issued a document that the debt had been settled and then found a witness to claim the opposite. Regarding the second claim that plaintiff Spirta made, the official document said that the incumbent government had nothing to do with it and that it instead concerned the personal relationship between Prince Miloš and the plaintiff.[28] It seems that this case was an attempt by plaintiff Spirta to take advantage of the change of government (Prince Miloš abdicated in June 1839) and make his alleged claims.

On 21 March 1852, the Court of the City of Belgrade ruled on a lawsuit of the plaintiff Jelisaveta Stefanović from Belgrade, against Aleksandar Marinović from Trieste, who was represented by Simo Stanisavljević. The lawsuit was conducted in order to exempt from sequestration the goods kept in Anka Jakšić's store, which were seized against the debt of Rufim Golemović. The document reveals that the case was before the Court of Appeals, which ordered the Court of the City of Belgrade to take certain circumstances into account. The Court of the City of Belgrade followed these instructions and accepted the following:

1) that the plaintiff proved by a contract of 20 June 1851 that Rufim Golemović had ceded all the goods in Anka Jakšić's store to the plaintiff, as the repayment of his debt amounting to 2,000 forints, in accordance with Article 884 of the Serbian Civil Code (SCC);
2) that the plaintiff bought the goods from a merchant who could sell them, so that the plaintiff, in terms of Article 221 of the SCC, was not obliged to abandon the goods, because she did not use any deception;
3) that the defendant's objection was not valid, to the effect that Golemović had no debt to the plaintiff, because he recognized his debt in a legally valid manner;
4) that the defendant's objection to the effect that this contract was concluded at the time of bankruptcy was not valid, because Golemović had not yet been declared bankrupt at that point, and this could not harm the plaintiff ("in the spirit of Article 917 of the SCC");

28 An act of 25 August 1842 filed with the Court of the City of Belgrade regarding the alleged receivables of plaintiff Georgij Spirta from ex-Prince Miloš (Archives of Serbia, Court of Appeal of Belgrade – Belgrade, no. 22, folder I (Arhiv Srbije, Apelacioni sud u Beogradu – Beograd, no. 22, folder I; hereinafter: AS, A-22, F I)).

5) that the objection that the sale of goods was made without an inventory could not be taken into account, because it was clear from the contract that it was a bulk sale, in accordance with Article 644 of the SCC.

Based on all the above, the Court of the City of Belgrade ruled that the goods in Anka Jakšić's store be exempt from seizure and become the plaintiff's property. The defendant was obliged to pay court fees within eight days from the date of receipt of the judgment. At its session on 11 June 1852, the Court of Appeals, Department I, upheld the judgment of the Court of the City of Belgrade.[29]

On 21 October 1859, the Court of Appeals, Department I, ruled on a dispute between the Čelebonović brothers, who were merchants, represented by a Đorđe (his last name is not legible in the document) and Andrija Dimitrijević, a tailor. The subject matter of the dispute was a debt of 485 groschen. The Court of Appeals embarked upon reviewing the judgment of the Court of the City of Belgrade in that case dated 13 August 1857. It ruled that the plaintiff's claim was not to be upheld because, in the opinion of the Court of Appeals, the plaintiffs admitted that the disputed debt had been paid to them.[30]

On 14 July 1860, the Court of Appeals decided in the second instance on the judgment of the Court of the City of Belgrade in the commercial litigation between Belgrade merchants Radovan Barlovac and Vojin Radulović, as one party to the proceedings, and Avram Gradištanac, the principal debtor, and Gile Vukojević, a guarantor, as the other party. The lawsuit was filed over a debt of 5,666 groschen. The first instance court failed to secure the presence of the principal debtor, Avram Gradištanac, at the hearing. The Court of Appeals noted that it was not able to make a decision, because the judgment did not cover the principal debtor. It returned all the documents to the Court of the City of Belgrade with a recommendation to interrogate the debtor and then act in conformity with the law.[31]

The case of Milan Mestanović's debts is an interesting one. Belgrade tailor Toma Stozlović sent a letter to the Court of Appeals, Department I on 7 September 1859. He asked for the repayment of a debt owed to him by the court's trainee, Milan Mestanović, worth 15 silver forints, to be achieved through the deduction of the requested amount from Mestanovic's salary. The debt was incurred on account of the tailor making pants and a vest for Mestanović. The tailor made an entry in

29 An excerpt from a trial before the Court of the City of Belgrade dated 21 March 1852; Confirmation of the Judgment by the Court of Appeals, Department I, at its session of 11 June 1852 (AS, A-22, F I, sh. 1–4).

30 Judgment of the Court of Appeals, Department I, of 21 October 1859 (AS, A-22, F I, sh. 1–3).

31 Decision of the Court of Appeals, Department I, of 14 July 1860; an act of the Court of the City of Belgrade, with an attachment entitled "List of Documents", sent to the Court of Appeals, Department I, dated 1 April 1859 (AS, A-22, F I, sh. 1–4).

his trading book, recording a bill amounting to 15 forints, which was recognized by the court. He then swore at the Court of the City of Belgrade that he properly maintained the trading book, told the truth regarding the debtor's personality and the value of the debt. The court officially confirmed the debt and issued a certificate of the oath. On this basis, the tailor asked debtor Mestanović to repay his debt on several occasions, but Mestanović refused to do so. Consequently, the tailor/creditor then approached the Court of Appeals where the debtor was employed, to collect the debt administratively, by garnishing it from the debtor's salary. In all likelihood, nothing happened regarding the salary garnishment, because a receipt issued by Toma Stozlović on 25 August 1860 shows that Mestanović's debt was paid by Marko Pavlović, a judge of the Court of Appeals. The same request for debt collection by means of salary garnishment against trainee Mestanović also came from the Ćuprija District Court. This court, in which Mestanović had previously worked, asked the Court of Appeals to deduct from his salary a total of 29 groschen, 22 for debt and 7 for court fees.[32]

4. Work on Commercial Legislation

4.1 The First Attempt 1849–1853

The Ministry of Finance believed that it was necessary to legally regulate trade in order to make progress. The Ministry found out that the Commercial Code for the Ottoman Empire had been published (or was about to be published) in Constantinople. In the first half of 1849, it asked the Ministry of Foreign Affairs to obtain a copy of that code, through the Serbian representative in Constantinople. The Ministry of Finance repeated the request the following April, in 1850, and said that it had not yet received a copy of the Commercial Code "for the entire Turkish Empire". Truth be told, they could not actually have received a copy because the Commercial Code for the Ottoman Empire was issued on 28 July 1850. Finally, a copy was received from the Ministry of Foreign Affairs on 11 December 1850, in French, under the title: "Code de commerce. Constantinople 1850. imprimmerie immperiale / Commercial Code in Constantinople 1850, in the imperial printing house./" There was also mention of the Bill of Exchange Code for the Austrian Empire dated April 1850, then of the fact that Wallachia and Moldavia had their

32 A letter by *Tomo Stozlović*, a tailor, to the Court of Appeals, Department I, dated 7 September 1859; an excerpt from the Register of the Court of the City of Belgrade dated 7 September 1859, with an invoice and a copy of the oath; a receipt of the collected debt of 25 August 1860; an act of the Ćuprija District Court sent to the Court of Appeals, Department I, of 22 September 1859 (AS, A-22, F I, sh. 1–4).

own commercial code and, additionally, that in Europe only Serbia did not have bill of exchange and commercial codes. All this can be read in the "Report on the Drafting of the Commercial Code in Serbia" of 30 December 1850, which was submitted by Jovan Gavrilović, Head of the Department of Trade at the Ministry of Finance.

In the Report, Gavrilović indicated that the Commercial Code for the Ottoman Empire contained the regulations: 1) on trade in general, on the establishment of trading companies, the bill of exchange law, and 2) on bankruptcy. He underscored that, unlike some other legislators, the Ottoman lawmaker had not passed regulations on maritime trade and on the organization of commercial courts (because the Ottoman structure of courts was different from the one in place in the country which was the role model). The author provided a detailed presentation of the contents of the Ottoman Commercial Code. He noted that the Ottoman Code contained legal norms which had already been drafted and proposed in Serbia. Thus, in the Draft Law on Civil Court Procedure, Chapter Ten regulated accounting disputes, Chapter XI bankruptcy, Chapter XII the debtor's arrangement with creditors, Chapter XIII the assignment of property. Gavrilović then provided references to help find the Russian Commercial Code, the French Commercial Code, the Austrian Bill of Exchange Code. Regarding the last one, he said that it was "printed with a Serbian translation in the supplements to Srpske novine of 18, 20 and 22 April 1850, issues no. 46, 47 and 48".

Gavrilović said that it was necessary to first decide which of the mentioned foreign commercial codes was to be taken as a model for the Serbian Commercial Code; only then should one proceed with the drafting of the code. From the space he dedicated to it and from his subsequent activity, it is obvious that rapporteur Gavrilović opted for the Ottoman Commercial Code. In Gavrilović's opinion, before embarking upon the drafting of the code, it was necessary to decide on the following: 1) whether ordinary courts would decide on bill of exchange and trade disputes, with the participation of one merchant, or 2) whether a single court would be established in Belgrade (as in Wallachia, which had only a single court based in Bucharest) or several commercial courts in several cities, 3) if a single court was established in Belgrade, whether it would adjudicate on all trade disputes in Serbia and whether its judgments would be enforceable, 4) if there were several courts, where they would be established and what kind of trade disputes they would resolve. Finally, the author wondered whether the future bill of exchange code should be applicable to all residents of Serbia or whether "certain classes of people should be exempted from it". He mentioned that soldiers, priests and farmers had previously been excluded from equivalent codes in Austria and that in Russia, pursuant to the applicable bill of exchange law, noblemen, soldiers, priests and farmers were exempted also. He suggested that Belgrade merchants and representatives of other guilds be consulted when resolving these issues.[33]

The Ministry of Finance adopted the report by Department Head Gavrilović and sent it to the Council on 25 January 1851. It put forward a proposal to set up a committee to answer the questions posed in the report.[34]

In its response, dated 8 February 1851, the Council recommended to the Ministry of Finance that a committee be established, comprising people who had a good understanding of trade, under the chairmanship of Jovan Gavrilović, to prepare the Draft Commercial Code. In its deliberations, the committee was supposed to adhere to the following guidelines given by the Council: 1) ordinary courts should adjudicate commercial litigation; 2) the Commercial Code should be drafted in a manner which ensured that the interests of domestic merchants, as well as their clients, were protected; and 3) the rigorous rules of the bill of exchange code should not apply to farmers and other people who were not engaged in trade.[35] On 22 February 1851, the Ministry of the Interior sent to the Council an act of the Administration of the City of Belgrade dated 30 December 1850. The Administration reported that merchants had held a meeting on 3 December 1850 under the auspices of the Belgrade authorities and requested the establishment of a commercial court for the city of Belgrade. This court would adjudicate undisputed claims in summary proceedings, without the right of appeal. The merchants were willing to develop a concept for the organization of that court.[36]

The Committee under the control of Gavrilovic prepared the Draft Commercial Code and sent it to the Ministry of Finance on 20 July 1851. The Ministry of Finance sent the draft to the Council on 19 September of that same year. The cover letter from the Ministry of Finance said that, besides Chairman Jovan Gavrilović, the members of the Drafting Committee were Cvetko Rajević, a member of the Supreme Court; Konstantin Cukić, Secretary General of the Ministry of Education and former professor of economics and finance at the Belgrade Lyceum; Svetozar Davidović, Secretary of the court department in the Prince's Office; Mihajlo Barlovac, Head of Department I of the Court of Appeals and former State Attorney; and merchants

33 Report on the Commercial Code by the Head of the Department of Trade, Jovan Gavrilović, to the Ministry of Finance of 30 December 1850 (AS, DS, 1853, 208, sh. 1–6). For more information about the work on the Commercial Code see: *Drakić, Gordana M./Stanković, Uroš N.*: Kodifikacija trgovačkog prava u Kneževini Srbiji (1849–1860), Zbornik radova Pravnog fakulteta u Novom Sadu, vol. 4 (2018), pp. 1577–1594.

34 Act of the Ministry of Finance sent to the Council on 25 January 1851 (AS, DS, 1853, 208).

35 Act of the Council to the Ministry of Finance dated 8 February 1851 (AS, DS, 1853, 208).

36 A Memorandum of the Ministry of the Interior to the Council dated 22 February 1851; an act of the Administration of the City of Belgrade sent to the Ministry of the Interior on 30 December 1850; a list of thirty-one Belgrade merchants who participated in the meeting on 3 December 1850 (AS, DS, 1853, 208, sh. 1–3).

Risto Veličković, Hadži Toma and Jovan Kumanudi. The official letter said: "This draft is based on the Commercial Code for the Ottoman Empire." It was mentioned that the Ottoman Commercial Code had a very similar content when compared with the commercial codes for the Kingdom of Greece and for the principalities of Wallachia and Moldavia. On that basis, it was concluded that the Serbian Commercial Code could, with the adoption of an Ottoman-style code, harmonize with the commercial legal frameworks of its close commercial and political partners. The Ministry of Finance considered that the draft Commercial Code should be submitted to the committee that reviewed the draft law on civil court procedure. They thought, with good reason, that the same committee should harmonize the subject matters of both codes, including over-indebtedness, claims against over-indebted parties, and the securing of loans which would otherwise be unattainable without organized courts and efficient judicial proceedings. Therefore, the Code of Civil Court Procedure was supposed to enter into force before or at the same time as the Commercial Code.[37]

"The Draft Commercial Code for the Principality of Serbia" had seven chapters:
Chapter I "On Merchants",
Chapter II "On Trading Books",
Chapter III "On Trading Companies",
Chapter IV "On Commission Agents",
Chapter V "On Sale and Purchase",
Chapter VI "On Bills of Exchange in General", and
Chapter VII "On Fees to be charged for Items falling within the scope of this Code".

The first six chapters of the Serbian Draft corresponded to the chapters of the Ottoman Commercial Code, with the title of the fifth chapter being different. The Serbian Draft had a total of 154 articles. The first six chapters, Articles 1 to 148, were almost identical to Articles 1–146 of the Ottoman Commercial Code. The Serbian Draft differed from the Ottoman Commercial Code in the following ways:

1) Article 3 was introduced, which stipulated that every merchant had to register his company with the locally competent first instance court.
2) Article 34 was different from Article 33 of the Ottoman Code.
3) Article 80 laid down in detail what was to be done, if the person receiving the bill of exchange was illiterate.
4) Article 97 stipulated that the bill of exchange that was full of the endorsers' signatures could be extended with an addendum.

37 Act of the Ministry of Finance to the Council of 19 September 1851 (AS, DS, 1853, 208, sh. 1–2).

5) Article 124 provided for a distance that required a day of walking as a reason for deadline extension (the Ottoman Commercial Code provided for six days of walking).
6) Article 125 defined different deadlines to file a lawsuit for a drawn bill of exchange, depending on the place where it was drawn – in Serbia two months, in the Ottoman Empire and in Wallachia and Moldavia four months.
7) Article 132 contained provisions on courts in Serbia where a bill of exchange could be appealed, unlike Article 130 of the Ottoman Commercial Code.

Articles 149–152 in the sixth chapter and Article 154 in the seventh chapter constituted the independent work of the Serbian legislative, taking into account the Serbian circumstances. The ban referred to in Article 150 of the Draft, prohibiting peasants (farmers), ordinary soldiers and non-commissioned officers from engaging in bill of exchange transactions was especially significant.[38] The Ottoman Code of 28 July 1850 was itself a product of comparative legal work, having been based on the French Commercial Code, taking into account specific Ottoman customs and traditions.[39]

On 9 September 1852, the Council sent the Draft Commercial Code to the Ministry of Justice, instructing it to appoint an expert to give his opinion on the draft. Dimitrije Crnobarac, Head of the Administrative Department of the Ministry, was selected. On 13 October 1852, he submitted a Report to the Ministry of Justice. The Report said that although the Draft Commercial Code contained substantive commercial law, it said nothing about the organization of commercial courts and the proceedings before them. Crnobarac proposed to resolve the issue of the regulation of commercial courts and the proceedings before them, as well as the relationship with civil court procedure. In conclusion, he said that merchants were keener on the regulation of the commercial court and the proceedings before it than on the subject matter of the Commercial Code per se. He believed accordingly that merchants would rather stake their claims in short, oral proceedings, which would be more efficient than in the pre-Code law. The Minister of Justice forwarded that report to the Council on 18 October 1852 and asked it to take the Draft Commercial Code into consideration as soon as possible.[40]

---

38 "Draft Commercial Code for the Principality of Serbia" (AS, DS, 1853, 208, sh. 1–24); *Padel, Wilhelm*: Das Handelsrecht, Wechselrecht, Konkursrecht und Seerecht der Türkei, in: Dove, Heinrich/Kohler, Josef/Meyer, Felix/Trumpler, Hans (eds.): Die Handelsgesetze des Erdballs, 3. Auflage, Band VIII: Süd-Europa II, Part Türkei, Berlin: R. v. Decker 1906, pp. 18–36.

39 *Padel, Wilhelm*: op. cit., pp. 7–8.

40 Report by *Dimitrije Crnobarac* to the Ministry of Justice dated 13 October 1852; an act of the Ministry of Justice to the Council of 18 October 1852 (AS, DS, 1853, 208, sh. 1–2).

The Council hesitated, which gave rise to dissatisfaction among merchants. The merchants sent a letter to Prince Aleksandar Karađorđević on 15 November 1852. They approached the Prince as the last line of defense against the threat of ruin accompanied by the loss of both honor and capital. The merchants first explained their perceived trading difficulties. In brief, as a consequence of the lack of a commercial code, merchants from the rest of Serbia were not keeping up with their debt payments to the merchants of Belgrade. Furthermore, Belgrade merchants were having to pay their debts to foreign, primarily Austrian merchants, in a timely fashion, abiding by the strict norms of Austrian commercial legislation. This was undermining lending activity, "and everyone knows that trade cannot be conducted without credit because credit is the soul of trade." Defaults on debts by merchants in the rest of Serbia were attributed to both prolonged and slow judicial proceedings (it often happened that a year would elapse before the undisputed debt was collected) and the necessity to bring actions against their debtors before the court of their place of residence, which created costs for them in terms of both money and time.

In their letter, the merchants complained that they had big problems with the repayment of debts by their debtors. The debtors abused the slow court procedure for collecting even undisputed debts. Debtors were not afraid of being sued in court; they knew that the prolonged court proceedings for the collection of receivables were conducted at the expense of their creditors. The loss of money and time for the creditor was usually significant, leaving the merchants in a humiliating position; they often had to "sit and watch the abuses of their debtors, flatter them and wait for them to pay the money they owed as some kind of charity".

Merchants recalled that trade, especially in Belgrade, was based on foreign loans, mostly from Austrian merchants. This meant that our Belgrade merchants were subject to the strict Austrian Commercial Code. They had to repay their debts at a precisely fixed time, without any objections whatsoever; if someone tried to avoid repaying the debt, they would be compelled to pay through the Austrian consulate and the Court of the City of Belgrade "or otherwise seal the shop". The merchants further stated that the National Bank in Vienna had reduced the loans to some of the Austrian creditors and completely terminated or cancelled to others, so that they were "no longer able to lend to our merchants ... Since all our trade and all our merchants are in someone else's hands, the Viennese developments shook up all the local merchants and made them heartsick."

The steps that could help, in the opinion of merchants, were the following:

1) A commercial code needed to be adopted, which would enable strictness and accuracy in the repayment of debts, quick adjudication and limit appeals in commercial litigation. 2) A single commercial court in Belgrade needed to be established for the entire territory of Serbia, which would have jurisdiction over all trade disputes in Serbia. Judgments of this court would be enforced within 24 hours and would not be appealable to the Court of Appeals. The only possible remedy

would be a review by the Ministry of Justice, at the request of one of the litigants. 3) A bank needed to be established, which could help local merchants in their times of need, "and which could save our merchants from ruin." Merchants suggested participating in the establishment of the bank with their contributions amounting up to 20,000 ducats. "This would free them from the yoke of foreign credit and millions of forints, instead of being paid to foreigners, would stay in the country." They also suggested that the bank be given money from the wards' properties, due to double benefits for both the wards (pupilla) and merchants.

At the end of the letter, the merchants pleaded with Prince Aleksandar and called upon him to save trade from ruin, and especially to help with the adoption of the commercial code, "because the law is the body and soul of trade, the law increases trade and the prosperity of our homeland and brings it into a state of flourishing." The merchants concluded their letter with a pathos-filled invitation to the Prince to resolve these issues, which would make his "glorious deeds" even more wreathed in glory and celebrated, not only by contemporaries but also by the "offspring".[41]

The addressee, Prince Aleksandar Karađorđević, saw the seriousness of the situation. On 23 January 1853, he ordered the Ministry of Finance to consider the requests of the merchants and submit a "draft" to the Council regarding "the best method" for the resolution of these requests. On 4 February 1853, the Ministry of Finance responded to Prince Aleksandar Karađorđević. A report on the work undertaken for the codification of the Commercial Code of 1849 was compiled by the Head of the Department of Trade, Jovan Gavrilović, Chairman of the Committee for the Drafting of the Commercial Code. He was the spiritus movens of the Commercial Code drafting process.

The author, Gavrilović, recalled that a year had elapsed since the submission of the draft commercial code by the Ministry of Finance to the Council for consideration. To the best of the Ministry's knowledge, the Council had not yet considered the draft. As indicated, the "complaint" of Belgrade merchants dated 15 November 1852 was well-grounded. He considered that "with the judicial proceedings as those we have in our country now, without a commercial code, without a bill of exchange system and without the establishment of a bank, even a small one, our trade cannot progress, and is destined to retrogress." He mentioned that "in the whole of Europe, the trading system is based on law, while in our country, little has been done by the Government for the promotion of trade." Finally, the Prince was kindly asked to transmit the "complaint" of the Belgrade merchants to the Council and order it to

41 Letter of Belgrade merchants to Prince Aleksandar Karađorđević of 15 November 1852 (AS, DS, 1853, 208, sh. 1–5).

consider the draft commercial code or to resolve the issues raised by the Belgrade merchants in another manner.[42]

This is exactly what Prince Aleksandar Karađorđević did in his letter to the Council of 11 February 1853. He made a recommendation to the Council to "seriously consider" the complaint by the merchants of 15 November 1852, as well as the report of the Ministry of Finance of 4 February 1853 with a view to improving trade and to inform him to that effect as soon as possible.[43] In its letter to Prince Aleksandar Karađorđević dated 29 July 1853, the Council said that it was in favor of the adoption of the Code of Civil Court Procedure and against the adoption of the Commercial Code.

The Council explained this in the following manner:

1) The Commercial Code had almost no practical value in the absence of special commercial courts and a special procedure in trade disputes.
2) The low educational level of the population prevented the application of the Commercial Code.
3) Furthermore, merchants were not trained to conduct trade in accordance with the rules set by the Commercial Code. That would inevitably lead to a reduction in the number of merchants, which would be bad for the country's economy.
4) The Council was of the opinion that the Code of Civil Court Procedure, land registers, the Criminal Code and the Criminal Procedure Code should be enacted before the Commercial Code, "as in other advanced countries", on the basis that a gradual development was preferable to a new regime imposed by force. Therefore, the Council believed that the Ottoman Commercial Code, drafted in the image of the French model, would remain "only a paper law" for a long time.

In the second part of the letter, the Council said that it had thoroughly considered both requests of the Belgrade merchants, of 3 December 1850 and 15 November 1852. The Council met the requests set out in the first act, related to the establishment of a special commercial court in Belgrade with short proceedings and without the right of appeal against its decisions. Accordingly, in its Draft Code of Civil Procedure, the Council proposed a faster way through which judgments could be handed down.

As for the second request of the Belgrade merchants of 15 November 1852, the Council examined each of its points in detail:

42 Letter of the Ministry of Finance dated 4 February 1853 to Prince Aleksandar Karađorđević (AS, DS, 1853, 208, sh. 1–3).

43 Letter of Prince Aleksandar Karađorđević to the Council dated 11 February 1853 (AS, DS, 1853, 208).

1) The Belgrade merchants complained because they had to file lawsuits against debtors before the local courts of the debtors, which was costing time and money. The Council concluded that Belgrade merchants could use a contractual clause to put merchants from the rest of the country under an obligation to accept that the Court of the City of Belgrade would have jurisdiction over potential disputes.
2) Regarding the complaints of the Belgrade merchants that trade lawsuits were prolonged, the Council was of the opinion that this was not true. It noted that the courts were very busy and the small number of lawsuits which were not concluded in during the year would be heard in the following! Similarly, the Council said that the arrangements in the Draft Code of Civil Court Procedure were aimed at shortening the proceedings.
3) The Belgrade merchants complained that they were paying their debts to Austrian merchants pursuant to the strict provisions of the Austrian Commercial Code, while their claims on merchants from the rest of Serbia were slowly adjudicated and collected. The Council recommended that the Belgrade merchants establish the same contractual relationship with merchants from the rest of Serbia as Austrian merchants had with them. More specifically, in their contracts with the Belgrade merchants, Austrian merchants stipulated that a dispute would be adjudicated by the Austrian court defined by the contract and that the judgment would be executed by the Court of the City of Belgrade. Accordingly, the Council suggested that the Belgrade merchants stipulate in their contracts with merchants from the rest of Serbia that the Court of the City of Belgrade would have jurisdiction in disputes, while the judgment would be executed by the district court for the place of residence of a merchant from another part of Serbia. The Council noted that the Belgrade merchants were not completely honest and did not tell the whole truth. The Council noted that foreign merchants, primarily Austrian ones, treated the Belgrade merchants as proper traders, that is, they would give them goods in quantities they requested, and at the appropriate trade margin, while Belgraders forced their goods on merchants from the rest of the country and took a higher percentage from them. On this point, the Council concluded that the adoption of the Commercial Code would not resolve the issue.
4) Regarding the complaint of the Belgrade merchants that the Viennese National Bank reduced loans to Austrian merchants, and then they passed it on to the Belgrade ones, the Council noted that it depended on the circumstances on the capital market and had nothing to do with the Commercial Code.
5) The Belgrade merchants were asking for the establishment of a single commercial court in Belgrade for the whole of Serbia. The Council noted that such an arrangement would certainly "be more convenient" to Belgraders. However,

since there were areas that were very distant from Belgrade, it would be more reasonable for that court to be "in the central part of the country".

6) The Belgrade merchants asked for a bank to be set up to help merchants by extending loans. The Council agreed with the request and recommended to the merchants that they undertake the task themselves, while the government would help with a deposit of 100,000 groschen, at a moderate interest rate. The Council did not accept the proposal to loan money from the wards' properties held by the courts to this bank. In the opinion of the Council, the wards' properties should be kept "as the most sacred bequest and protected from any danger".

The Council pointed out that it had considered the grievances of the Belgrade merchants seriously and for a long time. In the end, the Council concluded that the requests of the Belgrade merchants should be granted, in part, bearing in mind that the Code of Civil Court Procedure would be enacted and that some requests could not be met because they were ill-founded.[44] Prince Aleksandar Karađorđević accepted the opinion of the Council in its entirety and ordered the Ministry of Finance to inform the Belgrade merchants which of their requests had been taken on onboard and how they were to be brought about, as well as which requests had been denied, including the reasons for their non-acceptance.[45] This interrupted the work on the adoption of the Commercial Code.

4.2 Second Attempt 1856–1860

More than two and a half years later, on 12 March 1856, the Belgrade merchants sent a letter to Prince Aleksandar Karađorđević again. This long document was signed by 105 Belgrade merchants (by name or by the first letter of the name and their surname). They first reminded the Prince the importance of trade and "craftsmanship" for the development of any society and state. They then expressed the belief that "trade in our country, just like in other countries, can never survive, if not protected by the guarantees of a full-fledged commercial code." The Belgrade merchants recalled that they paid debts to their foreign creditors in accordance with the strict requirements of the relevant foreign commercial code, usually the Austrian Commercial Code. By comparison, the credit they gave to merchants from the rest of Serbia was not subject to such strict rules. The Belgrade merchants complained that the collection of their claims, including undisputed ones, had been postponed for years, even where there was a final and binding judgment.

---

44 Letter from the Council to Prince Aleksandar Karađorđević dated 29 July 1853 (AS, DS, 1853, 208, sh. 1–7).

45 Letter from Prince Aleksandar Karađorđević to the Council dated 11 October 1853 (AS, DS, 1853, 208).

The document went on to say that the good name and honor of the merchants were being exposed to danger. They alleged that many merchants had been ruined, lost their property and had their lives destroyed, as a result of the lack of an effective commercial code. The merchants further noted that export trade was facing similar problems. Exporters of locally produced items were not sure that the contract and the obligation arising from it would be fulfilled in time, "because the other contracting party – the local merchant – was unreliable", due to the fact that the courts were slow and inefficient.

As a result of the problems which had been brought to their attention, the Belgrade Municipality decided to consult with a committee comprised a number of the city's merchants. Together, they pleaded with the Prince and the government to issue a "full commercial code for our fatherland" in a timely manner. This code would, in addition to the provisions on commercial law, also contain provisions on the organization of commercial courts and a short procedure for resolving trade disputes, based on the principle of oral procedure.

In addition, the merchants put forward a proposal to set up a special commercial court in Belgrade. They also suggested that trade disputes in the rest of Serbia be tried by the existing district courts, pursuant to the Commercial Code and procedure. The proposed Belgrade Commercial Court would be a first level court, with its President, half of its judges and necessary staff appointed and funded by the government. The other half of the members would be elected by the merchants themselves from among their ranks and they would serve without remuneration. The commercial court would finally adjudicate disputes worth between 100 and 1,200 groschen. Disputes of higher value would be adjudicated by higher courts, but again pursuant to the Commercial Code and procedure.

The merchants requested for the future commercial code to accept the "principle of imprisonment of the debtor", who was not willing to pay his trade debt. It was explained in detail why it was not possible to use material security instruments to secure receivables in trade transactions (due to the speed of trading, due to the fact that often all the property of the merchants is capital or goods, and so on). It was mentioned that the debtor's imprisonment, as the last resort, was "recognized by the legislation of all states." The merchants requested for proceedings before commercial courts to be oral and, in accordance with the nature of trading, shorter, in comparison with ordinary litigation. This system should, so the merchants proposed, by run in the same manner as in "all well-organized" countries.

Up to its sixth page, the list of the merchant's requests dealt with the above matters related to commercial law. The document had twenty pages in total. Numerous issues were raised in the remainder of the text. First, the construction and improvement of means of transport were proposed: the construction of good roads; the introduction of the "stagecoach"; the cleaning of rivers for navigation purposes; two steamships on the Sava and the Danube; and improvement of the postal service.

Secondly, further reforms and demands were suggested, such as the establishment of a chamber of commerce; improvements in the commercial vocational education; the sending of young men to trade schools abroad; the introduction of Sunday and holiday schools; the improvement of Serbia's position between the Porte and European powers; the protection of proclaimed 'free land'; the introduction of land registers; and the creation of a professionalised legal framework for lawyers and notaries. For all practical purposes, this was a program for the modernization of the whole of Serbia.[46]

Precisely at that time, on 30 March 1856, the Paris Peace Treaty was concluded, which ended the so-called Crimean War (1853–1856). Russia was defeated by the Ottoman Empire, which was joined by Great Britain, France and Sardinia. Although Serbia did not take part in the war, provisions 28 and 29 of the Paris Treaty concerned Serbia's status. Certain self-governing privileges were confirmed: independent internal administration, freedom of religion, freedom of legislation, freedom of trade.[47] That treaty brought the Principality of Serbia, although still part of the Ottoman Empire, into a double connection with Europe: 1) instead of the Russian protectorate, Serbia's position was under the joint guarantee of European great powers; and 2) the Danube became an international river.

Due to these privileges, expectations were high. People talked about Serbia's great future in trade, saying that trading with the East would go through Serbia, that Belgrade would become the most important trading hub on the Danube. In anticipation of these developments, the Belgrade merchants were asking for the Europeanization of Serbian trade. They requested the adoption of a modern commercial code and the establishment of commercial courts, which would adjudicate lawsuits in accordance with new, special procedures. However, they were also asking for everything modern trade needed: good roads, an organised postal service, credit institutions, educated staff, a free and regulated market and efficient legal protection.[48]

On 21 March 1856, Prince Aleksandar Karađorđević wrote to the Council with respect to the renewed demands of the Belgrade merchants dated 12 March 1856. He said that "this case deserved serious attention of the Government" and recommended to the Council that they carefully consider all its aspects and propose measures to improve "trade and industry".[49] At its meeting on 4 April 1856, the Council set up a committee. The committee was tasked with comprehensively examining the requests of the Belgrade merchants and discussing when, how and by which measures they could be met. Some very reputable figures were invited to join

46 AS, DS, 1859, 960, sh. 1–11.

47 *Jovičić, Miodrag*: Leksikon srpske ustavnosti 1804–1918, Beograd 1999, p. 196.

48 *Jovanović, Slobodan*: op. cit., p. 92.

49 AS, DS, 1859, 960.

the committee: the chairman was Aleksa Simić and the members were Dimitrije Crnobarac, Atanasije Nikolić, Kosta Cukić and Jovan Gavrilović. The committee met on 20 and 21 April 1856. It drew up an extensive report of twenty-one and a half pages. The report was submitted to the Council on 23 May 1856. The Committee accepted the request to adopt a comprehensive commercial code, as well as short proceedings based on the principle of oral procedure and to set up commercial courts. It proposed the immediate establishment of a special committee for that job, whose work would be easier because the Draft Commercial Code, prepared in 1851, already existed.[50] On the other points, of which there were 14, the committee took a positive view, due to the convincing arguments put forward by the merchants.

In the end, the Committee pointed out: "Most of the state measures require funds, and only with them can something be done with more or less success." Serbia was economically lagging behind other European countries, substantial investment was needed to improve conditions for trade and economic activities. In order to secure the necessary funds, the Committee proposed to radically change the financial system, following the example of the more economically developed European countries. The government was criticized for neglecting this area and leaving it in its "original" state. According to the Committee, the reform of the financial system would lead to a severalfold increase in state revenues. This reform would be based on the idea of the wealthy paying their liabilities commensurate with the amount of their wealth. Liabilities would be eased for the more disadvantaged segments of the population. The Committee requested the Ministry of Finance to establish a separate committee to work on this reform, on the above basis.[51] The Council forwarded their decisions to the Prince's representative,[52] with a request to transmit it to all the ministries. It instructed the ministries to consider it and give their opinions, and the same thing was to be done by the Prince's representative.[53]

On 7 November 1856, the Minister of Justice and Education, Stefan Marković, replied that he "fully agreed with the opinion of the committee" with respect to the matters falling within the competence of his ministry. He pointed out that he supported the proposal which the committee made to the Council.[54] Two days later, in a lengthy document, he indicated that the Ministry of Justice and Education had

---

50 AS, DS, 1859, 960, sh. 1–11.

51 AS, DS, 1859, 960.

52 Under the Turkish constitution, there were ministers of the interior, finance and justice and education. In addition to them, there was the minister of the Prince's Office or the Prince's representative, who was in charge of affairs between the Serbian and the foreign authorities, so he was a kind of foreign minister. These ministers did not form a government; instead, each of them was independent in the performance of tasks falling within his purview and had a separate office.

53 Act of the Council to the Prince's Representative of 16 June 1856 (AS, DS, 1859, 960, sh. 1–3).

54 Act of the Minister of Justice to the Prince's Representative of 7 November 1856 (AS, DS, 1859, 960).

submitted to the Council a draft law on lawyers back in 1854, as well as a draft law on civil court procedure based on oral and short proceedings.[55]

The Ministry of Finance supported the proposal from the report of the committee in its entirety. It stated that it did not understand what the committee meant by the phrase "to change our financial system". The Ministry of Finance said that it had proposed changes to the taxation and budget systems, but that the overhaul of the entire financial system belonged "to those important tasks, which can only be accomplished gradually and through constant adjustment and improvement."[56]

Aleksa Simić, in his capacity as the Minister of Foreign Affairs, in his comment given on 19 November 1856, made a reference to two points from the report of the Committee, which concerned his ministry. The first was about the situation of the postal service. He said that the Serbian postal service cooperated well with the postal services of Wallachia and Turkey, while in the relations with Austria it was not possible to "achieve the desired result". The second point concerned the improvement of the agreement between the Sublime Porte and European powers with regard to privileges for Serbian trade. The Minister believed that his ministry could not do anything about it. He expressed hopes that the existing agreements would be changed by the contracting parties for the purpose of facilitating trade.[57]

In its document, dated 22 November 1856, the Ministry of the Interior supported the points concerning the construction of roads, the introduction of stagecoaches, the making of rivers navigable and the improvement of the postal service. It stated that it would prepare relevant draft laws on these issues and propose them to the Council. The Ministry pointed out that the vocational school of commerce should be reformed, a trade school should be established and that it was working on a draft law governing the sending of young men to learn crafts. It supported Sunday schools, the introduction of land registers and said that it was working on the matter. With respect to the issue of freedom of trade and crafts, it was of the opinion that the matter was within the competence of the Ministry of Finance.[58]

The office of the Prince's representative (which was also the Ministry of Foreign Affairs) collected all the opinions of the ministries and forwarded them to the Council on 24 November 1856.[59] In a letter to the Ministry of Finance, dated 8 January 1857, the Council ordered that in the process of working on a commercial

55 Act of the Minister of Justice to the Prince's Representative of 9 November 1856 (AS, DS, 1859, 960, sh. 1–3).

56 Act of the Minister of Finance to the Prince's Representative of 19 November 1856 (AS, DS, 1859, 960, sh. 1–2).

57 Act of the Minister of Foreign Affairs dated 19 November 1856 (AS, DS, 1859, 960, sh. 1–2).

58 Act of the Minister of the Interior to the Prince's Representative dated 22 November 1856 (AS, DS, 1859, 960, sh. 1–3).

59 Act of the Prince's Representative to the Council of 24 November 1856 (AS, DS, 1859, 960).

code for Serbia, the Draft Commercial Code which had been created in 1853, be considered first and foremost. A committee was appointed to work on the Commercial Code. The Council designated Jovan Veljković and Jeremija Stanojević as members of the Committee. Other members of the Committee were appointed by the Minister of Finance in agreement with other ministers.[60]

On 20 October 1857, Đorđe Đurić, the President of the Merchant Guild, sent a letter to the Council on behalf of all merchants. In that letter, he first mentioned the crisis and troubles in trade. He then noted the efforts of the state authorities to remedy the situation and finally repeated the request for the adoption of the Commercial Code. He referred to the draft which was stored in the archives of the Council and underscored the importance of the commercial code for Serbia in order to keep pace with well-organized countries and regulate the field of commercial law.[61]

In a letter to the Council dated 25 February 1858, the Minister of Finance mentioned the competence vested with the Board of Trade under Article 4 of its organisational rules. Specifically, the Board of Trade, as an elected tribunal, could adjudicate disputed cases in the fields of trade and crafts, entrusted to it by the parties. In that respect, the Board of Trade compiled Draft Rules on the basis of which the submitted cases would be admitted, investigated and adjudicated. The Ministry of Finance also sent the Draft to the Ministry of Justice. It then sent the Draft with comments to the Council for their consideration.[62]

That Draft consisted of three chapters and 28 articles. The first chapter "On the admission of litigation" in Article 1 stipulated that the Board of Trade, in its capacity as an elected tribunal, was to adjudicate only litigation of a commercial or artisan nature, with a minimum value of 1,000 groschen. Litigation of other types and of lower values would not be adjudicated. The litigants had to state their agreement in writing, declaring that they wanted their dispute to be decided by the Board of Trade and that they would be satisfied with its judgment. Then each litigant elected two elective judges from the list of members and deputy members of the Board of Trade. The president of the elected court was either the Chairman of the Board or chosen by the elected judges.

The second chapter "On the investigation of litigation" (Articles 8 to 19) in Article 8 set out that the Board of Trade was to act in accordance with "its common sense and in good conscience" when adjudicating cases. If one of the parties failed to come to the hearing without a justified reason, the Board of Trade could hand down a judgment on the basis of the presented evidence. If the litigant who was

60 Act of the Council to the Ministry of Finance of 8 January 1857 (AS, DS, 1859, 960, sh. 1–2).

61 Act of the Merchant Guild President, Đorđe Đurić, to the Council of 20 October 1857 (AS, DS, 1859, 960, sh. 1–2).

62 Act of the Minister of Finance to the Council of 25 February 1858 (AS, DS, 1859, 960, sh. 1–2).

absent failed to justify the absence within eight days from the hearing, the judgment was enforceable. Pursuant to the provision of Article 11 of the Draft, where both parties came to the hearing, the court would first hear the plaintiff on the disputed case and then the defendant. It would then examine the evidence submitted and hear witnesses. After such an investigation of the disputed case, it would pronounce a judgment with a clear conscience and common sense. The Board of Trade, as an elected court, could resolve litigations that arose from the following: a) trade and artisanal contracts; b) mutual accounts; c) debts on the books-records; d) bonded debts; and e) agreements reached on a sale or purchase, for which there is no evidence or proof. In cases where there were no elements to pronounce a judgment, the court determined which party should take an oath (Article 17). Persons sentenced to an oath would take it before one member of the elected court, at the first instance court with territorial jurisdiction (Article 18).

The third chapter "On resolving litigation" in its Article 20 provided that the president, four members of the court and the court recorder had to be present when resolving litigations. The judgment was passed by a majority vote. The judgment of the elected court had to contain the statements of the litigants, as well as the grounds for the judgment. The judgment had to be signed by the president, members of the elected court and the court recorder, certified by the Board's seal and issued to the litigants. A judgment drawn up and issued in this manner was immediately enforceable and could be sent directly to the executive authority for enforcement. The executive authority was under an obligation to enforce the judgment within eight days from the day of receipt. The judgments of the elected court were final and could not be appealed (Article 25). The losing party would pay to the Board of Trade a fee amounting to one thaler. The documentation on adjudicated cases was kept in the archives of the Board of Trade (Article 28).[63]

The Minister of Finance wrote to the Council on 14 May 1858, with regard to the new request by the Board of Trade and asked it to resolve as soon as possible the issue of the Draft under which the Board of Trade, as an elected court, would admit, investigate and adjudicate submitted cases. The Minister believed that considerably more time would be needed for the adoption of the Commercial Code and that a concept should be adopted according to which the Board of Trade would adjudicate as the elected tribunal.[64] In the end, that concept was not adopted. Instead, efforts were invested in the establishment of a commercial court. On 17 November 1859, the Minister of Justice, Marinko Radovanović, submitted two proposals to the Council. Their essence was that the Ministry of Justice, abiding by the wishes of the

63 The concept of the Board of Trade regarding the method of work of the elected court (AS, DS, 1859, 960, sh. 1–7).

64 Act of the Minister of Finance to the Council of 14 May 1859 (AS, DS, 1859, 960).

Malogospojinska (Nativity of the Most Holy Theotokos – Mother of God) Assembly and the Prince, had prepared a conceptual commercial court. The Commercial Court would replace the Court of the City of Belgrade, which had been adjudicating commercial litigations before that. The Court of the City of Belgrade would conclude the existing lawsuits, under the new name of the "Temporary Department of the Belgrade District Court". The cases not yet taken into consideration by the Court of the City of Belgrade and falling under the jurisdiction of the Commercial Court, would be transferred to the newly established Commercial Court. The Ministry of Justice considered this to be the best solution because otherwise the newly established Commercial Court would be immediately overwhelmed by a backlog of cases and would not be able to pay due attention to new cases.[65] This proposal of the Ministry of Justice was approved by the Council, as stated in the letter of the Council to the Prince dated 25 November of the same year.[66] On 1 December, the Prince confirmed the enactment entitled "Organization of the Commercial Court" and it was printed and published on 12 December 1859.[67]

The "Organization of the Commercial Court" of 12 December 1859 had 22 articles. Article 1 stipulated that, based on the identified need, a commercial court in Belgrade would be established. This court would have jurisdiction not only for the city of Belgrade, but also for the entire Belgrade district. Lastly, the court would rank as equivalent to district courts.

The Commercial Court in Belgrade was to consist of a president, one permanent member, the court secretary, a senior clerk, a court recorder (who also performed the duties of archivist and keeper of records), six regular members from among the ranks of the trade profession and their six deputies (also from the trade profession). Candidates for the president and the permanent member had to meet the same requirements as those for the appointment of district court judges, "and in particular he shall have completed legal sciences." The requirements for a regular member from among the ranks of the profession, or his deputy, included Serbian citizenship, 30 years of age, and that he had conducted trade honestly for five years. All members of the Commercial Court were appointed by the Prince by virtue of a decree, at the proposal of the Ministry of Justice. Members and their deputies from the ranks of the trade profession were elected by the assembly of Belgrade merchants, under the supervision of the president of the Court of the City of Belgrade. The president, the permanent member and the staff received salaries from the treasury, whereas members and deputies from the trade profession served without remuneration. The Court could sit if the President or the permanent member and three members

---

65 Two acts of the Minister of Justice to the Council of 17 November 1859 (AS, DS, 1859, 906, sh. 1, 1–2).

66 Letter of the Council to the Prince dated 25 November 1859 (AS, DS, 1859, 906).

67 Two acts of the Prince to the Council dated 1 and 12 December 1859 (AS, DS, 1859, 906).

or their deputies from the trade profession were present. The Court took decisions by a majority vote.

Under Article 16, the Commercial Court adjudicated: 1) all litigation related to contracts and settlements arising from trade between merchants, craftsmen and bankers; 2) all litigation related to persons involved in commerce; and 3) all those cases assigned to it by commercial laws or separate laws. The law defined a trade transaction as: 1) any purchase of food, goods and movables in general for the purpose of resale (whether in the given or in the processed form); 2) any contract or settlement arising from trade between merchants; 3) commission, sale and transportation "on land, on water"; 4) any procurement transaction, 5) banking transactions, 6) bill of exchange transactions; and 7) the undertaking of construction works. The Commercial Court tried bankruptcies involving commercial property.

In other district centres, besides Belgrade, commercial litigations would be tried by district courts, following the procedure defined for the Commercial Court. Each party to such proceedings could request the replacement of one of the district court judges by someone from the trade profession. Each district court was to prepare a list of 12 people from the trade profession "and other guilds" every year.[68]

In a letter to the Ministry of Finance, dated 26 November 1859, the Council stated that the National Assembly had proposed to the Council that the Bill of Exchange Law be passed as soon as possible. Therefore, the Council requested the Ministry of Finance to hear the Board of Trade on this issue and then submit to the Council its opinion and the opinion of the Board.[69] By virtue of an enactment dated 14 December 1859, Minister of Justice Marinko Radovanović submitted the Draft Commercial Code to the Council for consideration and approval.[70] The Council approved the Draft Commercial Code on 21 December, while the Prince did the same on 22 December 1859[71] and it was finally issued on 25 January 1860.[72]

---

68 "The Organization of the Commercial Court" of 12 December 1859 (AS, DS, 1859, 906).

69 Act of the Council to the Ministry of Finance of 26 November 1859 (AS, DS, 1859, 960).

70 Act of the Minister of Justice to the Council of 14 December 1859 (AS, DS, 1859, 960).

71 Letter of the Prince addressed to the Council of 22 December 1859; a letter of the Minister of Finance to the Council dated 6 February 1860 (AS, DS, 1859, 960).

72 "Commercial Code for the Principality of Serbia" of 25 January 1860 (AS, DS, 1859, 960).

Bibliography

1. Archival materials

ABH: Archiv Bosne i Hercegovine [Archives of Bosnia and Herzegovina in Sarajevo]:
VSS: Vrhovni sud za Bosnu i Hercegovinu – Sarajevo
ZVS: Zemaljska vlada za Sarajevo
AS: Arhiv Srbije [Archives of Serbia in Belgrade]:
A: Apelacioni sud u Beogradu – Beograd
DS: Državni savet – Beograd
BOA: Türkiye Cumhuriyeti Cumhurbaşkanlığı Devlet Arşivleri Başkanlığı Osmanlı Arşivi [Ottoman Archives of the President of the Turkish Republic's Office in Istanbul]:
A}MKT: Sadaret Mektubi Kalemi Evrakı
A}MKT.MHM: Sadaret Mektubi Mühimme Kalemi Evrakı
HR.MKT: Hariciye Nezareti Mektubi Kalemi Evrakı:
I.MVL: İrade Meclis-i Vala
T.MAT: Ticaret, Nafia, Ziraat, Orman, Meadin Nezareti
НБКМ–БИА: Национална библиотека "Св. Св. Кирил и Методий", Български исторически архив [Bulgarian National Library "St. St. Cyril and Methodius", Sofia, Bulgarian Historical Archive]:
F. 6: Fond 6 Hristo Tupchileshtov
НБКМ–ОС: Национална библиотека Св. "Св. Кирил и Методий", Ориенталски сбирки [Bulgarian National Library "St. St. Cyril and Methodius", Sofia, Oriental Collections]:
R 27: Колекция "Сиджили" [*Sicils* Collection]
Rs: Fond Ruse
Vd: Fond Vidin

2. Periodicals

Съветник [Counselor]: 1864
Bosansko-hercegovačke novine [Bosnian-Herzegovinian newspaper]: 1878–1883
Bosna [Bosnia]: 1874, 1875
Grazer Volksblatt [Graz People's newspaper]: 1882
Sarajevski list [Sarajevo's newspaper]: 1878–1883
Дунав/Tuna [Danube]: 1865, 1869, 1873, 1874, 1875, 1876, 1877
Държавен вестник [Bulgarian State Gazette]: 1897, 1899

3. Published primary sources

Allgemeines Reichs-Gesetz- und Regierungsblatt für das Kaiserthum Oesterreich, Jahrgang 1850, Erster Theil, Wien: K.k. Hof- und Staatsdruckerei, 1850.

Aristarchi, Grégoire: Législation ottoman ou Recueil des lois, règlements, ordonnances, traités, capitulations et autres documents officiels de l'Émpire Ottoman, vol. 1–6, Constantinople (Istanbul): Demétrius Nicolaïdes 1873–1881.

Bosnischer Boote pro 1901. Universal-Hand- und Adressbuch für Bosnien-Hercegovina, Sarajevo: In Comission bei der k. u. k. Hof-Buchdruckerei und Hof-Verlags-Buchhandlung Carl Fromme in Wien 1901.

Code de commerce de l'Empire Ottoman, Constantinople: Indicatore Bisantino 1850.

Das Ungarische Handelsgesetz. Deutsche Ausgabe, Budapest: Lafite & Elsner, 1876.

Düstur (Birinci tertip), vol. 1–3, [İstanbul]: Matbaa-i Amire 1289-1293 (1872/3–1876/7).

Gesetz- und Verordnungsblatt für Bosnien und die Hercegovina, Jahrgang 1907, Sarajevo: Daniel A. Kajon 1908.

Hristić, Nikola: Memoari 1840–1842, Beograd: Prosveta 2006.

Izvještaj o upravi BiH 1906, Zagreb: C. i Kr. Zajedničko ministarstvo financija, 1906.

Kanunname-i ticaret, [Istanbul]: Dar al-Ţibaah al-Amirah 1265 (1849).

Medželle i ahkjami šerije (Otomanski gragjanski zakon), Sarajevo: Daniela A. Kajona 1906.

Präjudicienbuch in Civilsachen, Band I, Obergericht für Bosnien und Hercegovina, Sarajevo 1899.

Präjudicienbuch in Civilsachen, Band II, Sammlung der Entscheidungen aus den Jahren: 1890, 1891, 1892, 1893, 1894 und 1895, Obergericht für Bosnien und die Hercegovina, Sarajevo 1899.

Salname-i Vilâyet-i Tuna, vol. 1–10, [Ruscuk]: Matbaa-yı Vilâyet-i Tuna 1285–1294 (1868–1877).

Salname-i Vilâyet-i Edirne, vol. 1–6, [Edirne]: Edirne Vilâyeti Matbaası 1287–1292 (1870–1875).

Sammlung der für Bosnien und die Hercegovina erlassenen Gesetze, Verordnungen und Normalweisungen, I. Band, Allgemeiner Theil, Wien: K.k. Hof- und Staatsdruckerei 1880.

Sammlung der für Bosnien und die Hercegovina erlassenen Gesetze, Verordnungen und Normalweisungen, 1878–1880, II. Band, Justizverwaltung, Wien: K.k. Hof- und Staatsdruckerei 1881.

Sammlung der Gesetze und Verordnungen für Bosnien und die Hercegovina, Jahrgang 1881 und 1883, Sarajevo: Landesdruckerei 1881.

Sammlung der Gesetze und Verordnungen für Bosnien und die Hercegovina, Jahrgang 1883, Sarajevo: Landesdruckerei 1883.

Sammlung der Justiznormalien für Bosnien und die Hercegovina, Band I, Jahrgang 1878–1885.

Sammlung der Justiznormalien für Bosnien und die Hercegovina, Band III, Jahrgang 1891–1895.

Vojdović, Mihailo (ed.): Srbija 1878, Dokumenti, Beograd: Srpska Književna Zadruga 1978.

Young, George: Corps de droit ottoman: recueil des codes, lois, règlements, ordonnances et actes les plus importants du droit intérieur et d'études sur le droit coutumier de l'Empire Ottoman, vol. 1–7, Oxford: Clarendon Press 1905–1906.

Zbornik zakona i naredaba za Bosnu i Hercegovinu, Godina 1881, Sarajevo: Zemaljska štamparija 1881.

Zbornik zakona i naredaba za Bosnu i Hercegovinu, Godina 1881 i 1883, Sarajevo: Zemaljska štamparija 1883.

Арнаудов, Христо: Пълно събрание на държавните закони, устави, наставления и високи заповеди на Османската империя, vol. 1–4, Tsarigrad (Istanbul): n.p 1871–1886.

Гранитски, Анастас: Търговско ръководство за тъгуване, промишленост, мореплавание и за търговски делания, Tsarigrad (Istanbul): T. Divitchiian 1858.

Попов, Стоил: Царски търговски законник, Ruschiuk (Ruse): Knigopechiatnitsa na Dunavskata oblast 1866.

Попов, Стоил/Чорапчиев, Иван: Турско-български писмовник, Ruschiuk (Ruse): Pechatnitsa na Dunavskata oblast 1868.

Петровићь, Ђорђе (ed.): Рѣчникь закона, уредба и уредбены прописа и пр. и пр. изданы у Княжеству Србіи одь 1827. до половине 1854. год., Beograd: Државна штампарија 1856.

Търговски закон, Sofia: Pridvorna pechatnitsa 1897.

Νικολαΐδης, Δημήτριος: Οθωμανικοί Κώδηκες, Constantinople (Istanbul): Eptalofos 1871.

4. Secondary literature

Ade, Mafalda: Ottoman Commercial Law and Its Application in Aleppo Province (1850–1880), in: Faroqhi, Suraiya/Veinstein, Gilles (ed.): Merchants in the Ottoman Empire, Leuven: Peeters 2008, pp. 243–258.

Ade, Mafalda: The Ottoman Commercial Tribunal in Damascus and the Use of Testimony and Evidence in Mixed Cases in the 19th Century, Quaderni Storici, vol. 51 (2016), no. 153, pp. 649–672.

Ajsner, Bertold: O općem građanskom pravu u Bosni i Hercegovini, Preštampano iz „Arhiva" za pravne i društvene nauke, Beograd: Štamparija Mirotočivi 1920.

Aličić, Ahmed S.: Uređenje Bosanskog ejaleta od 1789. do 1878. godine, Sarajevo: Orijentalni Institut u Sarajevu 1983.

Alunaru, Christian: Königreich Rumänien (1881–1947), in: Löhnig, Martin/Wagner, Stephan (eds.): Das ADHGB von 1861 als gemeinsames Obligationenrecht in Mitteleuropa, Tübingen: Mohr Siebeck 2019, pp. 283–304.

Alunaru, Christian: Ein nichtgeborenes Kind des rumänischen Zivilrechts in der Zwischenkriegszeit: Der Zivilgesetzbuchsentwurf Königs Karl II, in: Löhnig, Martin/Wagner,

Stephan (eds.): "Nichtgeborene Kinder des Liberalismus"? Zivilgesetzgebung im Mitteleuropa der Zwischenkriegszeit, Tübingen: Mohr Siebeck 2018, pp. 227–272.

Atar, Fahrettin: İflâs, İslam Ansiklopedisi, vol. 21, İstanbul: TDV Yayınları 2000, pp. 509–512.

Bağış, Ali İhsan: Osmanlı Ticaretinde Gayri Müslimler. Kapitülasyonlar-Beratlı Avrupa ve Hayriye Tüccarları (1750–1839), Ankara: Turhan Kitabevi 1983.

Bećić, Mehmed: Austrougarska reforma pravosuđa i građanskog postupka u Bosni i Hercegovini, Godišnjak Pravnog fakulteta u Sarajevu, vol. LVIII (2015), pp. 107–124.

Bećić, Mehmed: Das Privatrecht in Bosnien-Herzegowina (1878–1918): Zur Koexistenz österreichischer und ottomanischer Rechtsinstitutionen, in: Thomas Simon (ed.): Konflikt und Koexistenz - Die Rechtsordnungen Südosteuropas im 19. und 20. Jahrhundert, Band II, Serbien, Bosnien-Herzegowina, Albanien, Frankfurt am Main: Vittorio Klostermann 2017, pp. 71–136.

Bećić, Mehmed: Historijska i pravna osnovanost primjene Općeg građanskog zakonika u Bosni i Hercegovini nakon okupacije 1878. godine, Godišnjak Pravnog fakulteta u Sarajevu, vol. LIV (2011), pp. 63–79.

Bećić, Mehmed: Novi pogled na transformaciju šerijatskih sudova u Bosni i Hercegovini: da li je 1883. godine nametnut kolonijalni model primjene šerijatskog prava?, Godišnjak Pravnog fakulteta u Sarajevu, vol. LX (2017), pp. 59–82.

Bećić, Mehmed: Osmansko tanzimatsko pravo i austrougarski pravni poredak u Bosni i Hercegovini, Anali Pravnog fakulteta u Zenici, vol. 12 (2013), pp. 187–201.

Bećić, Mehmed: Pravni transplanti i pravni pluralizam: transformacija stvarnog prava u Bosni i Hercegovini 1878–1918, PhD thesis, Pravni fakultet Univerziteta u Sarajevu, 2018.

Bećić, Mehmed: Primjena Medželle u postosmanskoj Bosni i Hercegovini, Godišnjak Pravnog fakulteta u Sarajevu, vol. LVII (2014), pp. 51–66.

Bećić, Mehmed: Primjena Općeg građanskog zakonika u praksi Vrhovnog suda za Bosnu i Hercegovinu za vrijeme austrougarske uprave, master's thesis, Pravni fakultet Univerziteta u Sarajevu, 2013.

Boogert, Maurits H van den: The Capitulations and the Ottoman Legal System. Qadis, Consuls and *Beratlıs* in the 18th Century, Leiden: Brill 2005.

Bozkurt, Gulnihal: Batı Hukukunun Türkiye'de Benimsenmesi, Ankara: Türk Tarih Kurumu 2010.

Çağatay, Neş'et: Ribā and Interest Concept and Banking in the Ottoman Empire, Studia Islamica, vol. 32 (1970), pp. 53–68.

Cenić, Đorđe: Je li prekoračena suma određena budžetom na penzioniranje činovnika za 1874. god.?, Beograd: Državna štamparija 1876.

Čepula, Dalibor: Legal education in Croatia from medieval times to 1918: Institutions, courses of study and transfers, in: Zoran Pokrovac (ed.): Juristenausbildung in Osteuropa bis zum Ersten Weltkrieg, Rechtskulturen des modernen Osteuropa. Traditionen und Transfers, Band 3, Frankfurt am Main: Vittorio Klostermann 2007, pp. 81–152.

Çizakça, Murat: Comparative Evolution of Business Partnerships. The Islamic World and Europe with Specific Reference to the Ottoman Archives, Leiden: Brill 1996.

Čubrilović, Vasa (ed.): Istorija Beograda-devetnaesti vek, 2, Beograd: Prosveta 1974.

Davidova, Evguenia: Balkan Transitions to Modernity and Nation-States: Through the Eyes of Three Generations of Merchants (1780s–1890s), Leiden: Brill 2012.

Davison, Roderic: Reform in the Ottoman Empire 1856–1876, Princeton: Princeton University Press 1963.

Demirci, Akmandar: Osmanlı Devletinde Taşra Ticaret Mahkemeleri, PhD thesis, Ankara Üniversitesi 2019.

Dimitriu, Vasile/Gane, Stefan G./Flaischlen, Georg: Das Handels-, Wechsel-, Konkurs- und Seerecht Rumäniens, in: Dove, Heinrich/Kohler, Josef/Meyer, Felix/Trumpler, Hans (eds.): Die Handelsgesetze des Erdballs, 3. Auflage, Band VII: Süd-Europa I, Teil Rumänien, Berlin: R. v. Decker 1906.

Drakić, Gordana M./Stanković, Uroš N.: Kodifikacija trgovačkog prava u Kneževini Srbiji (1849–1860), Zbornik radova Pravnog fakulteta u Novom Sadu, vol. 4 (2018), pp. 1577–1594.

Ebert, Kurt: Die Pflege der Rechtsgeschichte an der Universität Graz im Zeichen der Historischen Schule, Zeitschrift der Savigny-Stiftung für Rechtsgeschichte, Germanistische Abteilung, vol. 87 (1970), pp. 239–286.

Eichler, Eduard: Das Justizwesen Bosniens und der Hercegovina, Landesregierung für Bosnien und die Hercegovina, Wien: K.k. Hof- und Staatsdruckerei 1889.

Ergene, Boğaç: Evidence in Ottoman Courts of Law: Oral and Written Documentation in Early-Modern Courts of Islamic Law, Journal of American Oriental Society, vol. 124 (2004), no. 3, pp. 471–491.

Findley, Carter Vaughn: The Tanzimat, in: Kasaba, Reşat (ed.): Cambridge History of Turkey, vol. 4 Turkey in the Modern World, Cambridge and New York: Cambridge University Press 2006, pp. 11–37.

Gedikli, Fethi: Osmanlı Şirket Kültürü: XVI.–XVII. Yüzyıllarda Mudârebe Uygulaması, İstanbul: Iz Yayıncılık 1998.

Georgewitsch, Andreas/Michajlowitsch, Stanoje: Das Handels-, Wechsel- und Konkursrecht Serbiens, in: Dove, Heinrich/Kohler, Josef/Meyer, Felix/Trumpler, Hans (eds.): Die Handelsgesetze des Erdballs, 3. Auflage, Band VIII: Süd-Europa II, Part Serbien, Berlin: R. v. Decker 1906.

Gerber, Haim: Muslim Law of Partnerships in Ottoman Court Records, Studia Islamica, vol. 53 (1981), pp. 109–119.

Gertscher, Adalbert: Das Handels-, Wechsel-, Konkurs- und Seerecht Von Österreich und dem Okkupationsgebiet Bosnien-Herzegowina, in: Dove, Heinrich/Kohler, Josef/Meyer, Felix/Trumpler, Hans (eds.): Die Handelsgesetze des Erdballs, 3. Auflage, Band XIII: Mitteleuropa II, Berlin: R. v. Decker 1906.

Hattenhauer, Hans: Europäische Rechtsgeschichte, 4. Auflage, Heidelberg: Müller 2004.

Hauptmann, Ferdo: Privreda i društvo Bosne i Hercegovine u doba austrougarske vladavine (1878–1918), in: Čović, Borivoj/Kovačević-Kojić, Desanka/Redžić, Enver (eds.): Prilozi za istoriju Bosne i Hercegovine, II, Akademija nauka i umjetnosti Bosne i Hercegovine, Posebna izdanja, Knjiga LXXIX, Odjeljenje društvenih nauka, Knjiga 18, Sarajevo: Akademija nauka i umjetnosti Bosne i Hercegovine 1987, pp. 99–211.

Ihsanoğlu, Ekmeleddin (ed.): Historija osmanske države i civilizacije, Istanbul and Sarajevo: IRCICA and Orijentalni Institut 2004.

Izmirlioglu, Ahmet: Ottoman Commercial Tribunals: Closer than Enemies, Farther than Friends, British Journal of Middle Eastern Studies, vol. 45 (2017), no. 5, pp. 1–20.

Jennings, Ronald: The Office of the Vekil (Wakil) in 17th Century Kayseri, Studia Islamica, vol. 42 (1975), pp. 147–169.

Jennings, Ronald: Limitations of Judicial Powers of the Kadi in 17th C. Ottoman Kayseri, Studia Islamica, vol. 50 (1978), pp. 133–172.

Jovanović, Aleksa: Postanak prvostepenog suda varoši Beograda, Beograd: n.p. 1904.

Jovanović, Slobodan: Ustavobranitelji i njihova vlada. Druga vlada Miloša i Mihaila, Sabrana dela, vol. 3, Beograd: BIGZ 1990.

Jovičić, Miodrag: Leksikon srpske ustavnosti 1804–1918, Beograd: Filip Visnjic 1999.

Juzbašić, Dževad: Neke karakteristike privredno razvitka Bosne i Hercegovine u periodu od 1878. do 1914. godine, in: Juzbašić, Dževad (ed.): Politika i privreda u Bosni i Hercegovini pod austrougarskom upravom, Akademija nauka i umjetnosti Bosne i Hercegovine, Posebna izdanja, Knjinga CXVI, Odjeljenje društvenih nauka, Knjinga 35, Sarajevo: Akademija nauka i umjetnosti Bosne i Hercegovine 2002, pp. 141–153.

Juzbašić, Dževad (ed.): Politika i privreda u Bosni i Hercegovini pod austrougarskom upravom, Akademija nauka i umjetnosti Bosne i Hercegovine, Posebna izdanja, Knjinga CXVI, Odjeljenje društvenih nauka, Knjinga 35, Sarajevo: Akademija nauka i umjetnosti Bosne i Hercegovine 2002.

Karćić, Fikret: Survival of the Ottoman-Islamic Laws in post-Ottoman Times in Bosnia and Herzegovina, in: Thomas Simon (ed.): Konflikt und Koexistenz – Die Rechtsordnungen Südosteuropas im 19. und 20. Jahrhundert, Band II, Serbien, Bosnien-Herzegowina, Albanien, Frankfurt am Main: Vittorio Klostermann 2017, pp. 43–70.

Kasumović, Amila: Austrougarska trgovinska politika u Bosni i Hercegovini 1878–1914, Sarajevo: UMHIS 2016.

Kenanoğlu, Macit: Ticaret Kanunnamesi ve Mecelle Işığında Osmanlı Ticaret Hukuku, Ankara: Lotus 2005.

Kessler, Daniel/Meites, Thomas/Miller, Geoffrey: Explaining Deviations from the Fifty-Percent Rule: A Multimodal Approach to the Selection of Cases for Litigation, Journal of Legal Studies, vol. 25 (1996), no. 1, pp. 233–259.

Krešić, Mirela/Pastović, Dunja: Königreich Jugoslawien (1918–1941), in: Löhnig, Martin/ Wagner, Stephan (eds.): Das ADHGB von 1861 als gemeinsames Obligationenrecht in Mitteleuropa, Tübingen: Mohr Siebeck 2019, pp. 219–282.

Kreševjaković, Hamdija: Dževdet-pašina pisma o Bosni iz 1864. godine, Sarajevo: Islamska dionička štamparija u Sarajevu 1932.

Kreševjaković, Hamdija: Iz bosanske trgovine XIX stoljeća, Narodna starina, vol. 1 (1922), no. 2, pp. 162–164.

Kreševjaković, Hamdija: Menafi – sanduci (Poljodjelske pripomoćne zaklade) u Bosni i Hercegovini (1866–1878), Narodna uzdanica, vol. IX (1941), pp. 23–41 (https://www.ibn-sina.net/images/pdf/znakovi/82/61_Hamdija_Kre%C5%A1evljakovi%C4%87_znakovi82.pdf, last access: 06.06.2021).

Kreševjaković, Hamdija: Stečajevi u Bosni 1867–1877, Narodna Starina, vol. 13 (1934), no. 34, pp. 189–192.

Kuran, Timur: The Absence of the Corporation in Islamic Law: Origins and Persistence, The American Journal of Comparative Law, vol. 53 (2005), no. 4, pp. 785–834.

Kuran, Timur: The Long Divergence. How Islamic Law Held Back the Middle East, Princeton and Oxford: Princeton University Press 2011.

Masheva, Ivelina: From Islamic Commercial Law to the French *Code de Commerce* – Oral And Written Evidences in Commercial Trials in Ottoman Bulgaria During the Tanzimat. Rechtskultur – Zeitschrift für Europäische Rechtsgeschichte, vol. 4 (2015), pp. 33–40.

Masheva, Ivelina: Ottoman Commercial Regulations during the Tanzimat period (1839–1877). Legislation Reforms and Their Application in the Town of Rusçuk, Papers of the American Research Center in Sofia, vol. 1 (2014), pp. 120–130.

Masters, Bruce: The Sultan's Entrepeneurs: The Avrupa Tüccarıs and the Hayriye Tüccarıs in Syria, International Journal of Middle East Studies, vol. 24 (1992), no. 4, pp. 579–597.

Matić, Dimitrije: Javno pravo Knjažestva Srbije, Beograd: Knjažestva Srbskog knjigopecatnji 1851.

Milkova, Fanny: Les traits caractéristiques et l'application du droit civil ottoman dans les terres bulgares au XIXe siècle, Bulgarian Historical Review, 1975, no. 4, pp. 26–37.

Milkova, Fanny: Influence du droit d'Europe occidentale sur le système juridique de Turquie, Bulgarian Historical Review, 1982, no. 4, pp. 92–97.

Mirković, Zoran S.: Pravne studije krajem XVIII i početkom XIX veka i beogradska Velika škola 1808–1813. godine, Anali Pravnog fakulteta u Beogradu, vol. 56 (2008), no. 1, pp. 126–149.

Mirkovic, Zoran S.: Die Anfänge des Rechtsstudium im Serbien der Neuzeit und die Juristenausbildung in der Habsburgermonarchie (ein Beispiel des Rechtstransfers), The Annals of the Faculty of Law in Belgrade – Belgrade Law Review, vol. 58 (2010), no. 3, pp. 151–162.

Özdeğer, Mehtap/Zeytinli, Emine: Ottoman Credit System and Usurers in Agriculture in the Nineteenth Century: Practices of Usury Contracts (Selem), Journal of Balkan and Near Eastern Studies, vol. 21 (2018), no. 5, pp. 594–612.

Padel, Wilhelm: Das Handelsrecht, Wechselrecht, Konkursrecht und Seerecht der Türkei, in: Dove, Heinrich/Kohler, Josef/Meyer, Felix/Trumpler, Hans (eds.): Die Handelsgesetze des Erdballs, 3. Auflage, Band VIII: Süd-Europa II, Part Türkei, Berlin: R. v. Decker 1906.

Pavlović, Stevan K.: Srbija-istorija iza imena, translated from English by Ivana Gazikalović-Pavlović, Beograd: Clio 2004.

Pavlowitch, Stevan K.: Serbia: The History Behind the Name, London: C. Hurst & Co. Publishers Ltd. 2002.

Pilar, Ivo: Entwicklungsgang der Rezeption des österreichischen allgemeinen bürgerlichen Gesetzbuches in Bosnien und der Herzegovina unter besonderer Berücksichtigung des Immobilienrechtes, Festschrift zur Jahrhundertfeier des Allgemeinen bürgerlichen Gesetzbuches, 1. Juni 1911, Erster Teil, Wien: Manz 1911, pp. 701–726.

Plagianakos, Georgios J.: Die Entstehung des Griechischen Zivilgesetzbuches, Hamburg: De Gruyter 1963.

Priest, George/Klein, Benjamin: The Selection of Disputes for Litigation, Journal of Legal Studies, vol. 13 (1984), pp. 1–55.

Rubin, Avi: Ottoman Nizamiye Courts: Law and Modernity, New York: Palgrave Macmillan 2011.

Rubin, Avi: Ottoman Judicial Change in the Age of Modernity: A Reappraisal, History Compass, vol. 7 (2009), no. 1, pp. 119–140.

Saracoğlu, Mehmet Safa: Letters from Vidin: A Study of Ottoman Governmentality and Politics of Local Administration, 1864–1877, PhD thesis, Ohio University 2007.

Schischmanow, Milan St./Subow, Peter A.: Das Handels-, Wechsel-, Konkurs- und Seerecht Bulgariens, in: Dove, Heinrich/Kohler, Josef/Meyer, Felix/Trumpler, Hans (eds.): Die Handelsgesetze des Erdballs, 3. Auflage, Band VIII: Süd-Europa II, Teil Bulgarien, Berlin: R. v. Decker 1906.

Schmid, Ferdinand: Bosnien und die Herzegovina unter der Verwaltung Österreich-Ungarns, Leipzig: Verlag von Veit & Comp. 1914.

Schön, Josef: Das bosnisch-herzegowinische, österreichische, ungarische und kroatische Handelsrecht in ihren Verschiedenheiten: ein vergleichender und ergänzender Kommentar zum Handelsgesetze für Bosnien und die Herzegowina, Wien: Manz 1913.

Shek, Adalbert: Uvod u predavanja o bosansko-hercegovačkom pravu, Mjesečnik Pravničkog društva u Zagrebu, vol. I (1914), no. 2, pp. 97–103.

Simon, Thomas: Thun-Hohensteinsche Universitätsreform und die Neuordnung der juristischen Studien- und Prüfungsordnung in Österreich, in: Zoran Pokrovac (ed.): Juristenausbildung in Osteuropa bis zum Ersten Weltkrieg, Rechtskulturen des modernen Osteuropa. Traditionen und Transfers, Band 3, Frankfurt am Main: Vittorio Klostermann 2007, pp. 1–36.

Sladović, Eugen: Islamsko pravo u Bosni i Hercegovini, Beograd: Geca Kona 1926.

Sladović, Eugen: Priručnik zakona i naredaba za upravnu službu u Bosni i Hercegovini, Sarajevo: Vlastita naklada izdavatelja 1915.

Streit, Georg/Diobouniotis, Georg: Die Griechische Handelsgesetzgebung, in: Dove, Heinrich/Kohler, Josef/Meyer, Felix/Trumpler, Hans (eds.): Die Handelsgesetze des Erdballs, 3. Auflage, Band VIII: Süd-Europa II, Part Griechenland, Berlin: R. v. Decker 1906.

Sućeska, Avdo: Vakufski krediti u Sarajevu prema podacima iz sidžila sarajevskog kadije iz godine 973, 974. I 975/1564,65 i 66., Prilozi za orijentalnu filologiju, vol. 44–45 (1996), pp. 99–132.

Tyan, Émile: Iflās et procédure d'exécution sur les biens en droit musulman (madhab hanafite), Studia Islamica, vol. 21 (1964), pp. 145–166.

Wallerstein, Immanuel/Kasaba, Reşat: Incorporation into the World Economy: Change in the Structure of the Ottoman Empire, in: Bacqué-Grammont, Jean-Louis/Dumont, Paul (eds.): Économies et sociétés dans l'Empire ottoman (fin du XVIIIe – début du XXe siècle), Paris: CNRS 1983, pp. 335–354.

Younis, Hana: Od dućana do pozorišta – sarajevska trgovačka elita 1851–1878, Sarajevo: Institut za historiju 2017.

Zobkow, Michael: Die Anwendung des allgemeinen bürgerlichen Gesetzbuches in Bosnien und der Herzegowina, Festschrift zur Jahrhundertfeier des Allgemeinen bürgerlichen Gesetzbuches, 1. Juni 1911, Erster Teil, Wien: Manz 1911, pp. 727–757.

Аврамова, Румяна/Василева, Весела/Генчев, Николай/Давчева, Даниела/Даскалова, Красимира/Димитрова, Дочка/Еленкова, Ваня/Куюмджиева, Миглена: Българска възрожденска интелигенция: Учители, свещеници, монаси, висши духовници, аптекари, писатели, издатели, книжари, търговци, военни... : Енциклопедия, Sofia: D-r Petur Beron 1988.

Андреев, Михаил: История на българската буржоазна държава и право 1878–1917, Sofia: Sofi-R 1993.

Андреев, Стефан/Велков, Аспарух/Груевски, Петко/Иванова, Светлана/Михайлова-Мръвкарова, Мария/Робев, Никола/Силянова, Емилия: Опис на османотурски документи за занаяти и търговия (XVI–XIX в.), Sofia: Narodna biblioteka "Sv. Sv. Kiril i Metodii" 1993.

Атанасова, Светла: Ролята на османското законодателство от средата на XIX век при изграждането на търговско-производствени структури в българските земи, Архив за поселищни проучвания, 2010, no. 1–2, pp. 37–62.

Габровски, М.: Организация на съдебната власт в България, in: 60 години българско правосъдие (1878– 1941). Юбилеен сборник, Sofia: Pridvorna pechatnitsa 1941, pp. 73–121.

Ганев, Венелин: Историческо развитие на несъстоятелността в главните негови моменти, Годишник на Софийския университет – Юридически факултет, vol. 10–11 1913/1914–1914/1915 (1915), pp. 8–216.

Ганев, Венелин: Историческото развитието на търговско право, Годишник на Софийския университет – Юридически факултет, vol. 12 1915/1916 (1921), pp. 1–275.

Джамбазов, Ангел: Правосъдната система на България 1878–1944, Sofia: Nauka i izkustvo 1990.

Дюмон, Пол: Периодът на реформите (Танзимат) (1839–1878), in: Мантран, Робер (ed.): История на Османската империя, Sofia: Riva 1999, pp. 472–535.

Манолова, Мария: Съдоустройствена система на Източна Румелия, Годишник на Софийския университет – Юридически факултет, vol. 66 (1975), pp. 43–55.

Машева, Ивелина: Българските търговци и правната регулация на търговско-финансовите отношения в Османската империя (40-те–70-те години на XIX в.), PhD thesis, Sofia University "St. Kliment Ohridski" 2015.

Машева, Ивелина: Правосъдието в провинцията – Видинският търговски съд в края на 60-те–нач. на 70-те години на XIX век, Балканите – език, история, култура, vol. 4 (2015), pp. 284–293.

Машева, Ивелина: Съдебни институции в областта на търговското право във Варна (40-те–70-те години на XIX век), in: Русев, Иван (ed.): Варна, българите и българските градове, Varna: Ongul 2016, pp. 75–92.

Милкова Фани/Андреев, Михаил: История на българската феодална държава и право, Sofia: Sofi-R 1993.

Новичев, Арон: Борьба между реформаторами и консерваторами в период Танзимата (1839–1853), Тюркологический сборник, 1973, pp. 82–108.

Новичев, Арон: История Турции, vol. 3, part 2, Новое Время (1839–1853), Leningrad: Izdatelstvo Leningradskogo universiteta 1973.

Паев, Костадин: Историята на българската държава и право и юридическото образование в България, Управление и образование, vol. 5 (2009), no. 3, pp. 202–214.

Панайотов, Николай: Гражданското съдопроизводство в залеза на Османската империя, Varna: Varnenski svoboden universitet "Chernorizets Hrabur" 1995.

Петров, Петър: Анкета за дейността на казалийските съдилища, Известия на Българското историческо дружество, vol. 37 (1985), pp. 441–453.

Тодоров, Николай: Балканският град XV–XIX век, Sofia: Nauka i izkustvo 1972.

Токушев, Димитър: История на новобългарската държава и право (1878–1944), Sofia: Sibi 2008.

Цекова, Снежана: Създаване на новобългарското търговско право, Ius Romanum, 2016, no. 1, pp. 887–900.

Шабанов, Фарух: О светских правовых нормах в законодателстве Османской империи периода реформ XIX в., Тюркологический сборник, 1978, pp. 180–186.